JEWISH ENCOUNTERS

Jonathan Rosen, General Editor

Jewish Encounters is a collaboration between Schocken and Nextbook, a project devoted to the promotion of Jewish literature, culture, and ideas.

>nextbook

PUBLISHED

FORTHCOMING

THE WORLDS OF SHOLOM ALEICHEM · Jeremy Dauber

ABRAHAM · Alan M. Dershowitz

MOSES · Stephen J. Dubner

BIROBIJAN · Masha Gessen

JUDAH MACCABEE · Jeffrey Goldberg

SACRED TRASH · Adina Hoffman and Peter Cole

THE DAIRY RESTAURANT · Ben Katchor

JOB · Rabbi Harold S. Kushner

ABRAHAM CAHAN · Seth Lipsky

SHOW OF SHOWS · David Margolick

MRS. FREUD · Daphne Merkin

DAVID BEN-GURION · Shimon Peres and David Landau

WHEN GRANT EXPELLED THE JEWS · Jonathan Sarna

MESSIANISM · Leon Wieseltier

The Eichmann Trial

DEBORAH E. LIPSTADT

THE EICHMANN TRIAL

NEXTBOOK · SCHOCKEN · NEW YORK

All rights reserved. Published in the United States by
Schocken Books, a division of Random House, Inc., New York,
and in Canada by Random House of Canada Limited, Toronto.

Schocken Books and colophon are registered trademarks of
Random House, Inc.

Library of Congress Cataloging-in-Publication Data
Lipstadt, Deborah E.
    The Eichmann trial / Deborah E. Lipstadt.
        p. cm.
    Includes bibliographical references.
    ISBN 978-0-8052-4260-7
    1. Eichmann, Adolf, 1906–1962—Trials, litigation, etc.
    2. War crime trials—Jerusalem 3. Holocaust, Jewish
    (1939–1945) I. Title.
KMK44.E33L57 2010   345.5694'420238—dc22   2010028620

www.schocken.com

Jacket illustration by Shannon Freshwater
Jacket images of the Eichmann Trial © Government Press
Office, State of Israel; Hannah Arendt © from the Jewish
Chronicle Archive / Heritage-Images / Imagestate
Jacket design by Barbara de Wilde
Printed in the United States of America
First Edition
2 4 6 8 9 7 5 3

DEDICATION

Much of the work on this book was done while I was the Judith B. and Burton P. Resnick Invitational Scholar at the Center for Advanced Holocaust Studies of the United States Holocaust Memorial Museum. My stay had all the ingredients scholars savor: outstanding colleagues, extensive scholarly resources, and the freedom to do one's own work. Then tragedy struck. At noon June 10, 2009, Special Officer Stephen Tyrone Johns, a long-term guard at the USHMM and a man beloved by the museum staff, saw an elderly man approaching the museum. Eager to be of help—this was his hallmark—Special Officer Johns reached out and pushed open the heavy glass door. Instead of entering, the man, an eighty-eight-year old racist, anti-Semite, and Holocaust denier, raised a rifle from beneath his coat and shot Stephen Tyrone Johns. He was murdered trying to do a kindness. Most mornings, including that day, when I arrived at the museum Special Officer Johns would be there. Often he would kid me about the piles of books I always had in tow. He seemed to have a friendly word for everyone. I had passed his station on my way to give a lecture a few moments before this incident and saw him at the door welcoming people to the museum.

The USHMM reopened two days later. The staff was

unsure if people would be too frightened to return. Shortly before the opening, I went outside to see if anyone was there. I fought back the tears when I saw the crowd. The line stretched around the block and down the street. It was significantly longer than for a normal June day. I heard people say that they were there in order to demonstrate that the bigots could not frighten them away. They had come precisely because the shooter wanted to keep them away. Visiting an institution dedicated to teaching about the Holocaust and fighting genocide had become an act of defiance.

It is with deep gratitude and sadness that I dedicate this book to the memory of Special Officer Johns and to the two officers whose quick response prevented this tragedy from assuming far greater proportions. Special Officer Johns's kindness and Special Officers Harry Weeks's and Jason "Mac" McCuiston's sheer professionalism are the hallmarks of this institution. We who were there, the thousands of people who visit on a daily basis, and the multitudes who benefit from its myriad of activities owe them and the USHMM's entire staff more than can be imagined. This is a very small token of that gratitude.

Deborah E. Lipstadt
June 10, 2010
Emory University
Atlanta, Georgia

CONTENTS

INTRODUCTION

In the early 1990s, when serving as a consultant to the team planning the United States Holocaust Memorial Museum, I attended a meeting of the Content Committee, the group of laypeople who reviewed the plans for the museum's permanent exhibition. It promised to be a spirited gathering. At issue was the question of displaying hair that the Germans had "harvested" from Jewish women at Auschwitz and sold to factories that produced blankets and water-absorbent socks for U-boat crews. When the Soviets liberated the camps, they found storehouses filled with hair. The Auschwitz Museum had given the USHMM a number of kilos of it. The museum designers planned to display it near a pile of victims' shoes, which also came from the camps. When the plan was first proposed, some staff members objected, arguing that it degraded and objectified the women. Although it was appropriate to display hair at Auschwitz, they did not think it should be displayed a continent away from there. Some feared that teenagers would find it, given the particular world that this age cohort often inhabits, ghoulishly amusing. Their opposition notwithstanding, the committee voted nine to four to display it. Then a number of survivors grew wary and asked that the matter be reconsidered; hence this meeting. The project director had come equipped with scholarly, psychological, and even rabbinic arguments to counter the opponents. Scholars, including one of the most eminent Holocaust historians—committee member Raul Hilberg—argued that the hair should be displayed because it demonstrated the Final Solution's "ultimate rationality." The Germans considered a body part something to be transformed into an "industrial object" and a salable commodity. Psychologists believed that the display of the hair would be no more disconcerting than many other aspects of the exhibit. Leading Orthodox rabbis determined that displaying it did not constitute a *nivul hamet*, desecration of the dead, and transgressed no religious rulings. In an attempt to allay some of the objections, the designers proposed that a wall be built in front of the exhibit case. Visitors would have to choose to see the display and not just happen upon it.

But then two committee members, both of whom were survivors, rose. One argued that this would be a "violation of feminine identity." A second spoke more personally. "That could have been my mother's hair. She never gave you permission to display it." When she sat down she said, in an aside, "It could have been *my* hair." The conversation soon ended. There was no vote, but all those present knew that the decision had been made. As we left, a committee member mused to no one in particular: "I don't object to the hair. But who am I to challenge survivors?" Shortly thereafter, the chair of the Content Committee announced that the hair would not be included in the permanent exhibition. Today it sits in a storehouse outside of Washington. It has never been displayed. Survivors, speaking in the first person singular, had a semantic, historical, and moral authority that trumped the psychologists, designers, historians, and other experts.[1]

But for the Eichmann trial, this might never have happened.

This trial, whose main objective was bringing a Nazi who helped organize and carry out genocide to justice, transformed Jewish life and society as much as it passed judgment on a murderer. In the general world it changed our perception of the victims of genocide.

On April 11, 1961, the theater of Beit Ha'am, Jerusalem's brand-new cultural center, was packed. Over seven hundred people filled the room for the trial of a man accused of being the chief operational officer of the Final Solution. Newspapers worldwide carried news of this event. American television networks broadcast special telecasts. This was not the first Nazi war-crimes trial. Yet there were more reporters in Jerusalem than had gone to Nuremberg. Why was this trial, coming just after the conclusion of Passover, different from the Nuremberg tribunals, where far more prominent figures in the Nazi hierarchy had been tried? Some of the differences were connected to the *when* of these two events. Nuremberg occurred in the immediate aftermath of the war, when many people wanted a mental respite from the horrors of the preceding five years. At Nuremberg multiple defendants had stood together in the dock. Now

one man stood alone. The drama of this proceeding was further intensified by the way Eichmann had been brought to
trial. Captured in Argentina, he had been spirited out of the
country to Israel. Even then, a full year after his capture,
there was still some mystery about precisely how he had been
found. But the *when* and the *how* of his capture were eclipsed
by the *who:* who found him and, more important, who would
try him. At Nuremberg victors had sat in judgment. Now
the victims' representative would sit in judgment. Immediately after the war, most Jewish Displaced Persons, as Holocaust survivors were once known, were focused on trying to
piece together a new life, not on seeking punishment. Even if
they had wanted to bring those who had destroyed their
world to justice, they had no mechanism to do so. In contrast, by 1961 the immediacy of the war and its consequences
had passed. The survivors, whose wounds had begun to be
bound up by the passage of time, now had more physical and
emotional stamina to demand justice. Most significant, however, now there was a sovereign entity to deliver it. The
State of Israel, which was then entering its Bar Mitzvah
year, exemplified the victims' emergence from the very powerlessness that had helped make the Final Solution possible.

The excitement and interest surrounding the trial had little to do with questions about its outcome. Most people,
both those in the courtroom and those beyond, expected
Eichmann to be found guilty. What was unknown was what
would happen when history, memory, and the law met in this
Jerusalem theater. Would the law prove adequate to adjudicate such an unprecedented event? Would the proceedings

deliver retribution or genuine justice? Would Eichmann's defense strategy of obedience to orders hold sway? Would he try to justify the genocide? And what, if anything, would be the lesson for the future?

As I complete this book, the fiftieth anniversary of the Eichmann trial nears. It is an event that is a vivid part of my childhood memories. During that period, dinner in our home was timed so that we could watch the televised news clips from Jerusalem. I remember the picture of Eichmann in the glass booth that appeared on the front page of *The New York Times* on the opening day. On the second day of the trial, if the Soviets had not launched Yuri Gagarin into space and safely retrieved him, the news of the trial would have been *the* lead story. As a thirteen-year-old, I was intrigued that something so profoundly connected with Jews had been featured so prominently. At this point in time, my world was pretty much divided into Jews and non-Jews. Virtually everyone in my immediate circle—classmates, neighbors, and friends—was Jewish. If you had asked me to recall those years, I would have told you about the thriving Jewish community in which I lived. And I would have insisted that I never encountered even a hint of anti-Semitism. I would have said so despite knowing that there were neighborhoods in which Jews could not live and firms that would not employ Jews. I had heard my friends' older siblings say that, despite their outstanding grades and academic records, they would not get into a particular Ivy League school because its

Jewish quota was filled. Already in the eighth grade we knew not to consider certain colleges because it was exceptionally difficult for a Jewish student who lived in a Jewish neighborhood and attended a Jewish school to gain admittance. Rather than being shocked by this, we accepted it, I am embarrassed to say, as a fact of life. This was how things were. In 1961, John Kennedy had just become president. I remember how perplexed I was during his fight for the Democratic presidential nomination by the media debate over whether a Catholic "could" be president. My twelve-year-old reasoning was straightforward: Everyone in America was either Christian or Jewish. It was a given that the presidency was off limits to Jews. White Christians, particularly those of privilege such as Kennedy, faced no such barriers. Why, then, should there be any question about his nomination? As I look back on those years, I am bemused, not by my failure to understand the difference between Protestantism and Catholicism, but by my acceptance that certain avenues were closed off to Jews. (My parents were far more incensed about it than I. In contrast, I was well aware and deeply troubled by the fact that African Americans faced terrible and violent discrimination.)

Into this simplistic and rather naïve world came the Eichmann trial and the Holocaust. It would take me a number of years to understand fully that the horrors for which Eichmann was being tried had sprung from the selfsame anti-Semitic soil that kept Jewish kids from top-notch schools, and Jewish graduates from jobs in many prestigious firms. Eventually I came to understand the interconnectivity of these phenomena. However, I never dreamed that from this soil would also come a movement that would have a dramatic impact on the course of my own life and would entrap me in a complex legal battle. My personal encounter with the Jew hatred which is at the root of Holocaust denial began with a few pages in my book *Denying the Holocaust: The Growing Assault on Truth and Memory.* I described David Irving, a British writer, as the world's leading Holocaust denier. Irving was a prolific author whose books were reviewed in *The New York Times, Times Literary Supplement,* and other prestigious publications. One of his books contended that Hitler did not know of the Holocaust and when he learned of it tried to stop it. After hovering at the edges of the denial movement for over a decade, Irving testified in 1988 at the trial of denier Ernst Zündel and declared that there was no "overall Reich policy to kill the Jews," that "no documents whatsoever show that a Holocaust had ever happened," and that gas chambers were "an impossibility."[2] He subsequently continued on that path in an unequivocal fashion. Explaining to a reporter why he had eliminated all references to the Holocaust from a new edition of his book on Hitler, he said: "If something didn't happen, then you don't even dignify it with a footnote." He denied the use of gas chambers to kill Jews systematically, argued that there was no officially sanctioned Third Reich plan to annihilate European Jewry, and contended that Hitler was "probably the biggest friend the Jews had in the Third Reich. He was the one doing everything he could to prevent nasty things happening to them."[3] Given his comments, I never imagined that I was doing anything potentially controversial when I described him in my book as a "Hitler partisan wearing blinkers" who "has been accused of skewing documents and misrepresenting data in order to reach historically untenable conclusions." I wrote that "on some level Irving seems to conceive himself as carrying on Hitler's legacy."[4] My comments were harsh but, given what he said, seemed quite legitimate.

In 1995, my book was bought by Penguin UK and published in the United Kingdom. Not long thereafter, I received a letter from Penguin's lawyers informing me that David Irving intended to bring a libel suit against me. I initially dismissed this as a groundless threat designed to frighten me. Even if his suit made it to court, which I doubted it ever would, I was certain the British justice system would see the absurdity of Irving's claims and dismiss the matter. I did not then realize that the United Kingdom's libel laws, which were the mirror image of American law, favored the claimant/plaintiff by putting the burden of proof on the defendant. The onus was on me to prove the truth of what I wrote, rather than on Irving to prove the falsehood. Another unique American safeguard was denied me. The public-figure defense is rooted in a United States Supreme Court ruling that a public figure, such as an author or a politician, can sue for libel only if he or she can prove malicious intent—i.e., that the author of the words knew or had good reason to know that they were false but wrote them anyway. This, too, would have prevented Irving from taking action against me in the United States. No such protections existed in the United Kingdom, and the matter came to court in 2000. After a trial lasting twelve weeks, the judge issued a three-hundred-page judgment which excoriated Irving and validated my defense team's claim that he was an unrepentant denier, falsifier of history, and someone who expressed overt racist and anti-Semitic views. Among the hundreds of people who made contact with me during this period were many survivors, who said that not since the Eichmann trial had they been so tied to a court proceeding. One older woman said: "I was shocked during the Eichmann proceedings by 'seeing' a mass murder. Now I am shocked, not just by the absurdity of a man with such a record dragging an established historian into court, but that the British courts are taking his claims seriously."

The British press paid careful attention to the case and the verdict. A number drew parallels with the Eichmann trial. *The Daily Telegraph* declared in its lead editorial, "This trial has done for the new century what the Nuremberg tribunals or the Eichmann trial did for earlier generations." Newspaper hyperbole aside, there was something else binding the two events. A few weeks earlier, the trials had been linked in a more overt fashion. During his trial, Eichmann wrote a memoir. After Eichmann's execution, Prime Minister David Ben-Gurion agreed, at the suggestion of prosecutor Gideon Hausner, to seal the manuscript in Israel's National Archives. Hausner contended that Eichmann had been given extensive opportunity to present his case, and therefore Israel had no further obligation to publicize his version of events. In the late 1990s, one of Eichmann's sons requested the release of the manuscript. A debate ensued as to what should be done. Some Israeli historians wanted a German research institute to annotate Eichmann's false assertions prior to publication. Other historians contended that Israel should just release the manuscript and allow the normal scholarly process to take its course. In the spirit of much else in the Middle East, nothing happened. During my trial, one of my former students suggested I look at the manuscript to determine if it contained anything that might be useful to my defense team. Our objective was to prove that Irving's claims about the Holocaust were lies. It was *not* to prove that the Holocaust happened. However, we thought that a direct statement from Eichmann's manuscript about the mass murders would, at the least, demonstrate that Irving denied the very things that those who had engaged in the killings freely admitted. Though it was a long shot, I asked my lawyer to request that Israel release the memoir. A few weeks later, I received a call from retired Israeli High Court Justice Gabriel Bach, who had served as Hausner's first assistant during the Eichmann trial. Bach told me that the current attorney general had consulted with a high-ranking group of jurists and historians and they had unanimously agreed that my request be honored. Even the prime minister had weighed in on the matter. The next day, my barrister, Richard Rampton, arrived in court carrying a small yellow computer disk with an electronic version of Eichmann's manuscript, which had just been downloaded to him. When Rampton, who as barrister had the task of pleading or litigating the case in court, introduced the contents of the disk as evidence, it was the first time the memoir was in the public's hand since Eichmann wrote it.

When I returned to my hotel that night, a hard copy of the manuscript was waiting for me. As I looked through it, I found myself comparing what I was experiencing to what had happened in Jerusalem in 1961. The importance of the Eichmann trial dwarfed mine. Irving cannot be compared to Eichmann in terms of either historical significance or the damage he caused to the Jewish people. Yet there were certain parallels between the two events. One of these men helped wiped out one-third of world Jewry. The second had dedicated himself to denying the truth of this. Neither man started his career expressing overt anti-Semitism. Both men seemed to me to have either conveniently adopted that ignominious mantle or let it emerge from where it had always been when it served their purposes. In the newly released memoir, Eichmann expressed himself as an inveterate Nazi and anti-Semite. In contrast to claims that would be made by Hannah Arendt that he did not really understand the enterprise in which he was involved, the memoir reveals a man who considered his Nazi leaders to be his "idols" and who was fully committed to their goals.

Most important, both *The State of Israel v. Adolf Eichmann* and *David Irving v. Penguin UK and Deborah Lipstadt* addressed phenomena that had a common source: anti-Semitism. Without centuries of this persistent hatred, the Third Reich would have found it impossible to mobilize hundreds of thousands of people to despise, scapegoat, and ultimately participate in the murder of European Jewry. (Could they have convinced countless people to take similar action against bicycle riders or redheads?) Holocaust denial would be impossible but for centuries of anti-Semitism. Deniers build their pseudo-arguments on traditional anti-Semitic stereotypes and imagery. They contend that Jews created the myth of the Holocaust in order to bilk the Germans out of billions of dollars and ensure the establishment of Israel. Once again the devious Jews have harmed innocent multitudes—Germans and Palestinians in particular—for the sake of their own financial and political ends. To someone nurtured by the soil of anti-Semitism, this makes perfect sense.

Yet, in a number of important ways, these two trials were diametric opposites. The most obvious contrast, of course, is that in Jerusalem the Nazi was the defendant. In London it was the Holocaust historian who was on trial. There is, however, an even more striking contrast. In Jerusalem testimony by the victims constituted the central element of the prosecution's case. Attorney General Hausner was determined that their voices should be heard in all their intensity. It was this decision by him, however questionable from a legal perspective, that gave survivors, such as the women I encountered at the meeting about displaying the hair in the Holocaust Museum, an iconic, almost mythic authority. In contrast, at my trial, we did not use survivors as witnesses. Though they inundated us with offers to testify, we eschewed their testimony for strategic reasons. Survivors would have constituted "witnesses of fact," attesting to the facts of what had happened. Because the Holocaust has the dubious distinction of being the best-documented genocide in history, we considered such testimony unnecessary. We did not want to suggest to the court that we needed witnesses of fact in order to "prove" the event. From the outset, one of my greatest fears was that my trial might become a "Did the Holocaust happen?" exchange. This is what had occurred during the trial of Holocaust denier Zündel. The court was transformed into a site for a debate over whether the Holocaust had happened. Zündel's lawyer challenged Holocaust survivors on the most minute details of their assertions. Holocaust historians found themselves having to defend the most basic fact. Historical nuance was mangled. Deniers testified for the defense and made all sorts of outlandish and historically unsubstantiated claims about the Final Solution. The newspapers and other media outlets reported the courtroom debates over whether there were gas chambers, whether Auschwitz had recreational facilities for the inmates, and other such historical absurdities. They treated deniers' claims as fact. Matters became so chaotic that the jury could not reach a decision and the case had to be retried. (At the retrial, the judge took "judicial notice" of the Holocaust, and this nightmare was avoided.) Had this occurred at my trial, I would have considered any victory I might have achieved to be Pyrrhic in nature. I knew we could demonstrate that every one of Irving's claims was bogus. We could show that Irving and, by extension, all deniers built their cases on inventions, distortions, and outright lies, and that the so-called evidence that they offered to prove their claims failed to do so. I worried, however, about a Zündel trial redux. Would labyrinthine courtroom exchanges with Irving about gas chambers and mass killings suggest to the general public that the existence of the Holocaust was something to be debated? I had read the transcript of Zündel's first trial. Distressed at how poorly both the Holocaust and history had fared in that courtroom, I lost sleep trying to imagine how the judge—there was no jury—would rule in mine. I feared that the miasma of denial might lead him to render a "split" decision. He might find for me but would use an "on the one hand, yet on the other hand" approach. I feared he might be befuddled by Irving's authoritative demeanor. I wanted an unequivocal and precise judgment. I believed the public had to be shown that denial was not an "other side," an "opinion," or a "view." My object was to demonstrate that it was a tissue of lies with no historical standing at all. My fears were for naught. The judge used the following terms to describe Irving's claims about the Holocaust: "perverts," "distorts," "misleading," "unjustified," "travesty," "reprehensible," and "unreal." Furthermore, the judge found that Irving's "falsification of the historical record was deliberate and . . . motivated by a desire to present events in a manner consistent with his own ideological beliefs even if that involved distortion and manipulation of historical evidence."[5] Our victory was sweeping. History had had its day in court and emerged triumphant.

One other thing linked these two events. I leave it for last because it discomfited me throughout the trial and continues to do so to this day. Ben-Gurion justified holding the trial in Israel because he believed that Israel, as the Jewish state, had the right to speak in the name of those who had been killed as Jews. Hausner had begun his opening statement by asserting that standing by his side were six million victims. When survivors heard of my coming legal battle, they sent me notes, letters, and copies of their books. All came with a similar message: "This is my story. This is what happened to me and to my family. This is what David Irving and his cohorts wish to deny. This is the history you must protect. You must stand up for us." I had never thought of what was facing me in such global and momentous terms. I saw myself as fighting a pseudo-historian who also engaged in overt racist and anti-Semitic expression. If I represented anyone, it was historians who wished to practice their craft and were willing to fight those who would abuse it for nefarious ends. However, as my trial approached, I found a larger meaning thrust upon it and upon me by survivors who were worried and frightened. I tried to reassure them that, even if I did not prevail, their history would be safe. They brushed aside my assurances. One survivor told me that he had attended a session of the Eichmann trial and hoped to come to mine. "Then the Nazi was in the dock. Now it is backwards." Now I see, as I look back, that this perhaps was for them a moment that meant the Eichmann trial and all it represented was ongoing. That the English High Court would be the venue for a Holocaust denier to spew lies and fabrications about things that had happened to them and had obliterated their families and the life they once knew seemed surrealistic at best.

Ironically, at the same time that they were investing what was facing me with such personal import, I was also receiving a very different message from other sources, particularly intellectuals and scholars in the field. Holocaust denial, they insisted, was the equivalent of flat-earth theory and, as such, was worthy of nothing more than utter ridicule. I should not, these skeptics insisted, take Irving's charges seriously. I was "silly," one leading historian opined, to invest so much time, effort, and resources into fighting them. "Just ignore it" was his sage advice. Though I agreed with these scholars about the total absurdity of denial, I explained that if I followed their advice, Irving would win by default. Because the British justice system placed the burden of proof on me, my failure to fight would result in a ruling that I was indeed guilty of libeling David Irving by calling him a denier. Irving could then legitimately interpret such a ruling as having concluded that his version of the Holocaust—no plan to kill the Jews, no gas chambers, no Hitler involvement—was legitimate. "So what?" the historian continued. "No one will believe it anyway." From my then budding awareness of the Internet, I knew he was wrong. There were many people who, though not fully accepting deniers' claims, might wonder if there was not some justification to Irving's positions.

Many British Jews did not want me to fight and pressured me to find some way "to settle this whole matter." Irving, they were convinced, would "win," irrespective of the outcome. "Even if he loses," one told me, "he will wrest so much publicity from the matter that he will end up ahead." Anthony Julius, my solicitor, the lawyer who prepared the case, developed the forensic strategy, and then turned it over to Richard Rampton to litigate in court, asked those who counseled me to settle what they thought my bottom line should be: Two million Jews? Three million? One death camp? Two or three? (Most dropped the matter at that point.) I juxtaposed these suggestions that I ignore the matter with the messages I was receiving from survivors. I could not look them in the eye and say, "When given the chance to stand up to this complete distortion of *your* history, I chose not to fight." These skeptics' arguments notwithstanding, I became convinced that I owed the survivors a full-fledged fight against those who would assault their history.

If I had any lingering doubts about my decision, they were erased for me on the first day of the trial. In front of a packed courtroom, Irving had spoken for three hours. Predicting a great victory for himself, he had repeatedly denied the Holocaust. I seethed with anger as I listened to the historical distortions and the anti-Semitism I found riddling his speech. When the session ended and we emerged from the courtroom, both of us were surrounded by reporters. He happily engaged them. I, however, was stymied. Because I was not giving testimony during the trial, my lawyers had asked me not to speak to the press. They did not want to antagonize the judge and give Irving room to say to him, "Lipstadt won't give testimony in your courtroom, but she was speaking on the BBC last night." I turned to my lawyer, who was standing next to me, and insisted that I should "give them something." He stood his ground: "Say nothing." As we debated the matter back and forth, an elderly woman worked her way through the crowd, approached me, touched me on the arm, and then rolled up the sleeve of her sweater. Pointing to the number tattooed on her arm, she said: "*You* are our witness." I forgot about talking to the press.

I never would have brought a matter of Holocaust denial to a court, but once I had been forced to enter that arena I had no choice but to respond with all my abilities. Though I did not represent the survivors, I felt their presence in that courtroom. They filled the public gallery. They gave me lists of the names of their murdered relatives. And when I prevailed, they embraced me, laughed, and cried with me. Though I'd never intended to do so, I ended up fighting for them.

In a larger sense, these two choruses of voices—those of the victims for whom evil is still present and the fight is still in some sense ongoing; and those who believe the battle has been won and that anti-Semitic horrors are the province of either the past or the "crazies" who are better ignored—still constitute the foundation upon which we build our understanding of Eichmann, the judgment against him, and his sentencing. Although some look back and see a trial of momentous importance because it brought to justice one of the key players in the Final Solution, others dismiss both the trial and Eichmann himself as things of little importance. They charge that Israel aggrandized the matter for political ends. They dismiss Eichmann as simply a transportation "specialist" and fault Israel for using the trial for Zionist ends. They claim he was a bureaucratic "clown," who really did not understand what he was doing. These differences of opinion about the Eichmann trial may well be metonyms for attitudes toward and perceptions of contemporary anti-Semitism. Some find the overt anti-Semitism of Holocaust deniers the ranting of idiots who are best ignored. Others take these comments quite seriously and see a dire and existential threat to Jewish well-being. They see a Holocaust-denying president of a large country, one that is poised to have nuclear weapons, occupying the podium of a world forum that was founded in the wake of the Final Solution with a mandate to stop genocide. They hear him deny the Final Solution and threaten the existence of the Jewish state. When they react strongly, they are cautioned by commentators and policy makers that they are overreacting or misunderstanding his charges. For them the issues that were adjudicated in Jerusalem are neither dead nor academic.

Historians often insist that they come to their research with a tabula rasa, that they judge each situation on its merits and do not let other matters shape their perceptions. In fact, no matter how much they may deny it, their personal experiences constitute facets on the prism through which their view of past events is refracted. For the sake of her readers and herself, a historian must acknowledge their presence and try to ensure that they clarify, rather than cloud, her understanding. And so, with my own encounter with history, the law, the study of the Holocaust, and raw anti-Semitism as a backdrop, I began to explore what happened in Jerusalem five decades earlier.

The Eichmann Trial

1

On the afternoon of May 23, 1960, members of Israel's Knesset were gathered for what promised to be a run-of-the-mill budget debate. Then Prime Minister David Ben-Gurion rose, walked to the podium, and, speaking with what *The New York Times* described as "dramatic understatement," began a two-sentence announcement that sent shock waves around the globe:

> I have to inform the Knesset that a short time ago one of the great Nazi war criminals, Adolf Eichmann, the man responsible together with the Nazi leaders for what they called the Final Solution, which is the annihilation of six million European Jews, was discovered by the Israel security services. Adolf Eichmann is already under arrest in Israel and will be placed on trial shortly under the terms of the law for the trial of Nazis and their collaborators.[1]

Providing no further details, Ben-Gurion departed, leaving behind a stupefied parliament. After a few moments of silence—estimates differ radically—the room erupted. People wept, hugged, and marveled: Eichmann *b'yadenu*, Eichmann is in *our* hands. On the street, similar scenes ensued. People crowded around radios and newspaper kiosks seeking details. The historian Tom Segev compared the emotions that swept the country to what had happened twelve years earlier. "Israelis had not known, since the Declaration of Independence, so deep a sense of national unity." Israel's half-million survivors had a more alloyed response. Warsaw Ghetto fighter Yitzhak (Antek) Zuckerman voiced these contradictory emotions: "Joy and sadness have alighted upon us, entwined with each other." This strange mix of emotions was exemplified by the verse from Psalm 94 which the editors of the profoundly secular newspaper *Maariv* chose to headline the story: *"El nekamot hofea,"* "The Mighty God to Whom Vengeance Belongs Has Appeared."[2]

This was the second time Eichmann had been captured. Immediately after the war, the Allies had apprehended and interned him in a POW camp. Using a pseudonym, he hid his identity. Then a number of Nuremberg defendants connected him to the Final Solution. They testified about his unrelenting quest to murder as many Jews as he could and his pivotal role in the annihilation process. Assuming that he was now on the Allies' radar screen, Eichmann feared that they would soon uncover his true identity, or that another prisoner, in an attempt to curry favor with his captors, would expose him. With help from other former SS officers who were POWs, he escaped and headed to a remote area of Germany, where a lumber company provided work and shelter for many war criminals. When the company went bankrupt, he decided to leave for Argentina, where other Third Reich officials had found a warm welcome. Their wartime résumés did not impede their entry into the country. With the help of Catholic officials who had the imprimatur of high—if not the very highest—Vatican offices, Eichmann obtained a Red Cross passport and, using the pseudonym Ricardo Klement, made his way to Buenos Aires.[3]

Eichmann's escape was facilitated by the fact that at this time no one who had the requisite resources or legal authority was interested in finding him. After the Nuremberg tribunals, the Allies, worried about the Cold War, lost their ardor for hunting Nazis and alienating their new ally, West Germany. Israel, fearing annihilation by the Arabs, focused on protecting live Jews, not avenging dead ones. Germany's chancellor, Konrad Adenauer, whose government was riddled with former Nazis, had declared the hunt for war criminals over.

Eichmann's whereabouts would probably have remained a mystery but for a combination of amateur sleuthing and dumb luck. Two of the names most prominently associated with locating him had little to do with the operation, whereas those who played a pivotal role have largely been forgotten. The Nazi hunter Simon Wiesenthal and, to a lesser degree, Tuvia Friedman have claimed and been given credit over the years for finding Eichmann. In fact, though they may have been responsible for finding other murderers, they contributed relatively little to this capture. These two men were among a small group of survivors who believed that the Nazi war criminals had to be tracked down and punished. They devoted their lives to this effort, chasing down Nazis when most other agencies had lost interest. Wiesenthal has claimed that his information led to Eichmann's "capture, conviction, and execution."[4] In his memoirs he described how he thwarted Vera Eichmann's attempt in 1947 to have her husband declared dead, ostensibly so that she could be eligible for a widow's pension. He claimed to have discovered that the person who supposedly witnessed Eichmann's death was Vera's brother-in-law and informed the occupation authorities of this fact. They immediately rejected her petition. Wiesenthal touted this as the most important step in the hunt, because a death declaration would have ended efforts to find him. (Who looks for a dead man?) Actually, it is highly unlikely that the Israelis who eventually apprehended Eichmann would have been waylaid by a death certificate obtained by his family. More important, however, Wiesenthal's claims conflict with what he said at the time. In a January 1960 letter to the Israeli ambassador in Vienna regarding this incident, Wiesenthal explicitly stated that the petition was rejected "at the instigation of the authorities" and made no mention of his supposed role. In another letter to the ambassador, written around the same time, Wiesenthal noted: "Mrs. Eichmann has a sister in Prague, whose husband is a government official. Name to follow." In other words, he did not seem to know the family's name, yet he subsequently claimed to have exposed their efforts to have Eichmann declared dead.[5]

In 1952, Vera and her sons disappeared overnight, leaving all their possessions behind. No one—neighbors, teachers, or officials—apparently knew they were leaving. Her relatives claimed she had left to remarry. This "dead of night" departure convinced Wiesenthal that Vera had reunited with Eichmann. He thought, however, that they were somewhere in northern Germany. Wiesenthal's suspicions were aroused again when he saw a death notice for Eichmann's mother listing Vera Eichmann as a mourner. Why would a remarried widow use the name of her former husband? All these were important indications that Eichmann was still alive, but they were not what led to his capture. One important lead did come into Wiesenthal's hands early in the 1950s. Baron Mast, a fellow Austrian stamp-collector, told Wiesenthal that Eichmann was in Argentina. Six months later, Wiesenthal passed the information on to the World Jewish Congress, who gave it to the CIA. No one followed up. The Israelis, whom Wiesenthal also informed, failed to follow up.[6] Had any of these groups acted, Eichmann might have been found and Wiesenthal would have deserved the credit. Wiesenthal's claim to have found Eichmann is further weakened by his letter to the Israeli ambassador to Austria written on September 23, 1959, about six months before Eichmann's capture. In it he suggested that Eichmann could be found in northern Germany. The lesser-known but no less indefatigable sleuth Tuvia Friedman also spent great energy and resources in trying to track down Eichmann. After the capture, he claimed to have provided the Israeli government with the crucial information on his whereabouts. He did give them Eichmann's address in Argentina, but by the time he did so, Israeli officials already knew of Eichmann's whereabouts and were making plans for his capture.[7]

Wiesenthal's aggrandizement of his role in the Eichmann capture is far less disturbing and historiographically significant than another of his inventions. In an attempt to elicit non-Jewish interest in the Holocaust, Wiesenthal decided to broaden the population of victims—even though it meant falsifying history. He began to speak of eleven million victims: six million Jews and five million non-Jews. Holocaust historian Yehuda Bauer immediately recognized that this number made no historical sense. Who, Bauer wondered, constituted Wiesenthal's five million? In fact, this figure is too high if one is counting victims who were targeted exclusively for racial reasons, but too low if one counts the total number of victims the Nazi regime killed outside military operations. Among those specifically targeted to be killed by the Nazis on racial or ideological grounds were Germans with mental and physical disabilities, some of the Roma (also known as Gypsies), Soviet and Polish educated and leadership elites, and Soviet civilians of certain ethnic groups. Many others, including domestic political opponents, members of national resistance movements in occupied territories, German homosexual men, and Germans labeled as "asocial" were imprisoned or sent to concentration camps. Countless died as a result of the atrocious treatment to which they were subjected. They were not, however, targeted for complete annihilation. Some historians speculate that, had the Germans won the war, the remainder of the Roma and other groups, including those of mixed, "Aryan" and Jewish, heritage, would have been eventually been totally annihilated. The Germans would probably have also liquidated millions of civilians of certain ethnic groups (Russians, Belorussians, and "Asiatics" of the Soviet Union). Ultimately, had the Germans had a free hand to carry out these genocides, the number of victims would have dwarfed that of the Jews. The motivation for this intended mass murder was clearly racial. However, while the Germans wanted to eliminate these groups, it was the Jew that they considered the most *immediate* and *dangerous* enemy. In the Nazi mind it was Jews alone who had the nefarious capacity to organize other subhuman racial groups into opposing Germany. Killing *all* Jews—irrespective of age, location, education, profession, religious orientation, political outlook, or ethnic self-identification—was *the priority* in the race war that Nazi Germany conducted. This, rather than the numbers, the means, and the racial motivation, is what was unique about Nazi policy toward the Jews. Wiesenthal admitted to Bauer that he had invented a historical fantasy in order to give the Holocaust a more universal cast and to find a number which was almost as large as the Jewish death toll but not quite equal to it. When Elie Wiesel challenged Wiesenthal to provide some historical proof that five million civilian non-Jews were murdered in the camps, Wiesenthal, rather than admit that he invented the five million number, accused Wiesel of "Judeocentrism," being concerned only about Jews.[8]

Wiesenthal's historical invention obscures, if not denies, the true nature of the Holocaust. Wiesenthal's invented equivalencies ride roughshod over the history of Nazi policy during 1941–44. Unfortunately, in many circles it has become accepted wisdom. At the first Holocaust memorial commemoration in the Capitol Rotunda, both President Jimmy Carter and Vice President Mondale referred to the "eleven million victims." Carter also used Wiesenthal's figures of "six million Jews and five million others" in his Executive Order establishing the United States Holocaust Memorial Council. I have attended Holocaust memorial commemorations in places as diverse as synagogues and army forts where eleven candles were lit. More significant is that strangers have repeatedly taken me and other colleagues to task for ignoring the five million non-Jews. When I explain that this is an invented concept, they become convinced of my ethnocentrism. However well meaning, this fraudulent effort on Wiesenthal's part will have far more lasting deleterious implications than his confusing stories regarding his Nazi hunting.[9]

Who, then, did find Eichmann? Actually, the decisive information came from three unlikely characters. Lothar Hermann, a nearly blind German half-Jew, had fled to Argentina in 1939, after spending some time in a concentration camp. Fearful of the numerous Nazi sympathizers in Argentina, he hid his Jewish identity. He was so successful at this subterfuge that the second character in this episode, his teenage daughter Sylvia, who apparently knew nothing of her Jewish heritage, was comfortable dating the son of a former Nazi officer. The third critical player was Fritz Bauer, a Jewish lawyer from Stuttgart who had been incarcerated in concentration camps but was able to flee Germany during the 1930s. He stayed in Denmark until the Germans invaded it, and then spent the rest of the war in Sweden. After the war, though well aware that "former" Nazis filled many important posts in Adenauer's government, he did something many people—Jews in particular—found incomprehensible, if not reprehensible. He not only returned to Germany but accepted a governmental appointment as attorney general of Hesse. His colleagues were Germans who had loyally served the Third Reich and had then seamlessly shifted their loyalty to the Federal Republic. (Showing amazing adaptability, some of these judges and attorneys had preceded their service to the Third Reich with service to the Weimar Republic.) Bauer tolerated this because he wanted to help rebuild a legitimate judicial system in Germany and bring Nazi war criminals to justice.

One day in the late 1950s, Sylvia Hermann introduced her new boyfriend, Klaus Eichmann, to her family. Though Adolf Eichmann had established a false identity, the children had kept his name. Klaus boasted to Sylvia's family that his father had been a high-ranking Waffen-SS officer and declared that the Germans should have finished the job of exterminating the Jews. Though Lothar was appalled, he was intent on not revealing his Jewish identity and therefore maintained his silence. But for an article that subsequently appeared in *Argentinisches Tageblatt*, the story might have ended there. Describing Germany's preparations for its first major war-crimes trial, the German-language Argentinian newspaper mentioned Eichmann as one of the criminals still at large. When Lothar was read the article, he recalled the remarks made by Sylvia's boyfriend and suspected that the young man was Adolf's son. His suspicions were further aroused by the fact that Klaus had been vague about his father's fate and had refused to give Sylvia his address, forcing her to correspond with him through a mutual friend. Aware that the German Embassy in Buenos Aries was staffed by former Nazis, Lothar chose not to share his suspicions with them. In fact, these German officials may well have known that Eichmann was present in Argentina, given that his sons and wife were there on German passports. Instead of turning to the embassy, Lothar wrote to the Frankfurt prosecutor's office, which was handling the case. His letter landed on Fritz Bauer's desk. Intrigued, Bauer asked Hermann to ascertain Eichmann's address. The Hermanns devised a scheme. Sylvia went to the run-down neighborhood where Klaus lived and asked around until she located the Eichmann home. At this rather ramshackle house she was greeted by a middle-aged man who identified himself as Klaus's uncle and invited her to wait for Klaus to return. She chatted with him about her schoolwork, love of languages, and future plans. Upon his return, Klaus immediately suggested he take her to the bus. As they were leaving, he bade the man farewell, addressing him as "Father." The young couple parted at the bus stop. Had Klaus discovered her intentions, she could easily have been harmed by the local neo-Nazi and right-wing groups with which the Eichmann boys were associated.[10]

Upon receiving the address from the Hermanns, Bauer felt further investigation was warranted. He was reluctant to turn to the German security services, or to his colleagues in the judicial system, because he suspected that they harbored Nazi sympathies and might warn Eichmann. He decided that, even though he was a member of the West German judicial system, he would give this information to Israel and allow its security services to investigate. Bauer had the support of the minister-president of Hesse, Georg August Zinn, whom he informed about his efforts. Bauer's decision may have been based, in great measure, on Argentina's dismal record regarding Nazi war criminals. A few months earlier, German authorities had told the Argentines that there was good reason to believe that Dr. Josef Mengele was in their country and that they wanted to extradite him. Argentinian authorities claimed—probably falsely—that they did not know where he was. Moreover, they told the Germans, since his crimes had been political, he was ineligible for extradition. In the interim, Mengele disappeared.[11]

The information about Eichmann reached Isser Harel, the head of Israel's security services (Mossad). Preoccupied with other security issues, he did not consider this a matter of utmost urgency. After a lapse of four months, Harel asked an Israeli operative who happened to be in Argentina to check the address. The agent walked through the neighborhood and decided that, given its dilapidated state, this could not be home to a high-ranking Nazi official who had once had access to Jews' possessions. When Bauer learned of this lackadaisical approach, he insisted that Harel send agents posing as German officials to meet Hermann personally. They could then assess the quality of his information.

Harel again let a few months pass, then asked an agent who was going to be in Argentina on other business to visit Hermann. The officer went to the Hermanns' home and was nonplussed to discover that their informant was blind. He was inclined to dismiss the entire matter until he spoke with Sylvia, whose detailed description of her encounter with Klaus's "uncle" intrigued him, and he asked them to continue sleuthing. The Hermanns checked the property records for Eichmann's address and discovered that the land was owned by an Austrian named Schmidt, but that the utility bill went to a Ricardo Klement. Hermann concluded that Schmidt was Eichmann and proposed an outlandish theory about Eichmann's having had plastic surgery to disguise his appearance. The Israelis easily discovered that Hermann's theory was wrong and dropped the case. The issue might have died here but for Bauer, who in the interim had learned from another source that Eichmann, now known as Klement, was in fact living in Argentina.[12]

At this point, Tuvia Friedman, who had devoted his life to finding Nazis, inadvertently almost sabotaged the effort. In 1959, having heard that Eichmann was in Kuwait, he released the information to the press. It generated headlines worldwide. Bauer and the Israeli agents feared it might alert Eichmann that he was being sought and cause him to flee or adopt a new identity.[13]

In December 1959, Bauer was scheduled to visit Israel. Furious at Harel's lack of resolve, he complained to Attorney General Haim Cohen, who summoned Harel to a meeting. After lambasting Israel's efforts and declaring that a second-rate German policeman could have done better, Bauer informed Harel that yet another informant had linked Eichmann to Klement. Given that the same information had come from two separate sources, Harel's attitude changed immediately. Shortly thereafter, he dispatched the Mossad's chief interrogator, Zvi Aharoni, to Argentina to confirm Eichmann's identity.

Aharoni obtained pictures of Eichmann and confirmed that he and Ricardo Klement were one and the same. When Ben-Gurion learned of this, he immediately decided that Eichmann should be apprehended and brought to Israel to stand trial. Having received a green light from Ben-Gurion, Harel assembled a group of "volunteers," almost all of whom just happened to be members of or closely connected to the Israeli security services. Using false papers, they entered Argentina, leased houses, rented cars, tracked Eichmann, and devised a plan. They quickly discovered that the Eichmann family had moved to an even more modest abode. This cinder-block house, which they had built themselves and which had no electricity or running water, was situated on a secluded bluff on Garibaldi Street. Eichmann may have chosen the spot because anyone who approached could easily be seen. Yet, even though the seclusion allowed for privacy, it also eliminated the possibility of neighbors' giving the Eichmanns warning.

Each night, Eichmann took the bus home from his job at a Mercedes-Benz assembly plant. He alighted at a stop a couple of hundred meters from his home. On May 11, 1960, the Israelis parked two cars midway between the bus stop and his home. One had its hood up. The men assigned to grab him huddled over the engine as if they were checking a mechanical failure. The second car parked down the road, facing the first car. When Eichmann neared the "disabled" car, the driver of the second car switched on the headlights, effectively blinding him. Peter Malkin, a hand-combat specialist and one of the agents near the "disabled" car, jumped him. While they struggled, Eichmann emitted what Malkin described as "the primal cry of a cornered animal."[14] Eichmann was bundled into one of the cars and taken to a "safe house." Other members of the team had remodeled the house in order to create an internal room to hold the prisoner. Harel, who was in Buenos Aires supervising the operation, was informed that all had gone off without a hitch. Using a code, he cabled Ben-Gurion that Eichmann was in their hands.

Unbeknownst to the Israelis, the operation had not been the total success that they assumed. The Argentinian secret police were apparently aware of Eichmann's identity and had been keeping close tabs on him. On the night of the kidnapping, an undercover agent was tailing him. He saw three men grab, subdue, and bundle Eichmann into a car. The police agents followed the car to the safe house where he was held. The secret police were also aware that, a few days before the kidnapping, a contingent of Israelis had arrived in the country and were engaged in some sort of surreptitious activity. Apparently, this much-touted secret action was anything but a secret.[15] If the Argentines were indeed aware, one has to wonder why they did not abort the operation. Could they have been relieved that he was being taken off their hands?

At the safe house, Eichmann's captors searched their prisoner to make sure that he was not hiding a cyanide capsule. Then they matched his physical characteristics—head size, scars, and eye color—to the information contained in the file Bauer had given them. Everything matched except for the dental records: the SS officer of the file had his full set of teeth; the captured man wore dentures. Some of the members of the Israeli team were taken aback to discover that, rather than a haughty SS officer living in splendor, they had caught a trembling factory worker in shabby underwear with false teeth. They were also struck by how mind-bogglingly obedient he was. At one point Malkin and one of his colleagues took Eichmann to the toilet. They waited outside. After a few minutes, Eichmann called out to Malkin, *"Darf ich anfangen?"* ("May I begin?") Only when told yes did he begin to move his bowels. Witnessing Eichmann's behavior, Aharoni wondered if this man could possibly have "decided the fate of millions of my people." Aharoni conducted the interrogation.

"Name?" "Ricardo Klement," the name he used in Argentina.

Your previous name? "Otto Heninger," the alias he used in Germany.

What is your Nazi party number? "889895," the number in the file.

What is your "SS number"? "45326," the other number in the file.

Then Aharoni repeated his initial question.

"Name?"

"Adolf Eichmann."

The hunt was over.[16]

2

Eichmann's captors still had to get him out of the country. Harel arranged for an El Al plane, which was due to bring an Israeli delegation to the celebration of Argentina's 150th anniversary, to carry a few extra passengers on its return to Tel Aviv. On May 20, shortly before the scheduled departure, the doctor on the team drugged Eichmann, leaving him groggy but compliant. His captors dressed him in an El Al uniform. Phony identification papers had been prepared for him by the team's master forger. Together with some of his captors, who also donned El Al uniforms, they piled into a car and headed for the airport, where the Britannia turbojet stood ready to depart. If airport security asked about the dazed man's condition, they would be told that he had overindulged while on leave. The plan proceeded smoothly, and just past midnight the plane lifted off and headed not toward Recife, as the official flight plan indicated, but to Dakar, Senegal. Harel did not want to risk having the Argentines ask Brazilian authorities to waylay the flight in order to stop the kidnapping. This would be the longest stretch a Britannia had ever flown. When it landed, twelve hours later, it was flying on fumes. During the flight, the captain informed the crew that the semicomatose man in first class was Adolf Eichmann. They responded, as would much of

Israel a few days later, with amazement, satisfaction, and, for those who had lost family, pain. El Al's chief mechanic, who Harel had insisted accompany the flight in case of equipment problems, had seen his parents murdered by the Nazis. At age eleven, he had futilely tried to save his six-year-old brother. Upon learning the mystery passenger's identity, he began to weep. When an Israeli security man handed Eichmann a cigarette, the mechanic exclaimed: "You give *him* cigarettes. He gave *us* gas." Later, having composed himself, he slipped into the first-class section and sat staring at Eichmann.[1]

As soon as the plane taxied to a corner of Lod Airport, Eichmann was taken to prison and Harel went to brief Ben-Gurion. Shortly thereafter, Ben-Gurion made his dramatic, but terse, announcement. Israeli officials provided no further details on Eichmann's kidnapping. However, within a few days the operation's secrecy was breached. *Time* magazine provided an exceptionally detailed and generally correct description of how Israeli operatives had waylaid Eichmann in Buenos Aires, bundled him into a car, and flown him out of the country on an El Al plane. Argentinian police agents who had seen the abduction and knew where he was being held were probably the source of the information. They may not have intervened because of those in the government who were happy to let the Israelis take him off their hands. However, now that the news was public, Argentina played the aggrieved party and demanded details.

Israel responded with what has been described as one of the more undiplomatic notes in diplomatic history. Mixing half-truths with fiction, it asserted that "volunteers" who happened to be Israelis had "established contact" with Eichmann and inquired whether he would come to Israel for trial. After he "spontaneously" agreed, they brought him to Israel and turned him over to the authorities. Israel had been "ignorant" of these details until Argentina demanded an explanation and an investigation was conducted. The nine-hundred-word note—a tome by diplomatic standards—also took a swipe at Argentina by observing that it was home to "numerous Nazis." Foreign diplomats dismissed the explanation as "flagrantly unbelievable." Even the Israeli ambassador to Argentina described it as *"bobe meises"* (fiction). The far-fetched story and the reference to "many Nazis" intensified Argentina's anger. In a thinly veiled comparison to Nazi Germany, Argentina responded by describing the Israelis' actions as "typical of the methods used by a regime completely and universally condemned." Attempting to salvage Israel's good relations with Argentina, Ben-Gurion crafted a personal letter to President Frondizi, in which he hewed to the myth of the "volunteers" but apologized for their violation of Argentina's sovereignty. He beseeched Frondizi to understand that a trial in Israel would be "an act of supreme historic justice."[2]

Frondizi, pressured by Argentinian nationalists who were livid at the breach of their country's sovereignty, ordered Argentina's UN representative, Mario Amadeo, to take the matter to the Security Council. Amadeo, a Catholic nationalist who had supported Franco, Mussolini, and the Axis, demanded Eichmann's return and, using unvarnished language, compared Israel's actions to lynchings and mob violence. Israel, he declared, threatened world peace and security. Equating Jews who fled the Nazis with Nazi war criminals who fled punishment at the end of the war, he observed that not just Eichmann, but Jewish refugees had also benefitted from his country's liberal admissions policy. Had Argentina been more vigilant, he mused, it might have ensnared not only Eichmann but also these Jews. Again equating victim and victimizer, he lauded his country's open door to those "flee[ing] persecution." His comments infuriated Israel's foreign minister, Golda Meir, who described Amadeo's linkage of Eichmann with his victims as "quite extraordinary." She found the notion of Eichmann "flee[ing] persecution" striking. Eichmann's captors, she observed, could have lynched him "on the nearest tree." Instead, they turned him over to face justice. She apologized for their actions but asked whether the "threat to peace" was posed by Israel's actions or by "Eichmann at large, Eichmann unpunished."[3]

Initially, most Security Council members, including the United States, supported Argentina's repatriation demand. However, attitudes changed when the Soviet Union intimated that it might call for reconvening the Nuremberg tribunals, as was its right. In an attempt to resolve the matter, U.S. Ambassador Henry Cabot Lodge declared that Argentina's demand for "reparation" had been fulfilled by

Meir's apology. The other members agreed. As one pundit observed, Argentina got an apology and Israel got Eichmann. Apparently, Lodge's compromise resulted from more than just Cold War politics. Richard Nixon "suggested" to Lodge that if he was still interested in being his vice-presidential candidate, he find a resolution that was less hostile to Israel and recognized Eichmann's crimes.[4]

Given that both Israeli and Argentine officials knew precisely what had happened and Argentina had not tried to prevent the Israelis from leaving with Eichmann, this debate was rather farcical. While many Argentines protested the violation of their country's sovereignty, others were prompted to ask why their country had become the "favorite refuge" for Nazis such as Eichmann. *La Prensa* declared Eichmann "human scum." In *El Mundo*, the prominent Argentine writer Ernesto Sabato asked, "How can we not admire a group of brave men who . . . had the honesty to deliver him up for trial by judicial tribunals instead of . . . finish[ing] him off on the spot?" *La Razón* reminded readers that the man whose abduction Argentina was now protesting had in 1944 sent fourteen hundred Jews with Argentinian passports to Bergen-Belsen. Even papers that protested the violation of Argentina's sovereignty acknowledged that Israel's reference to "numerous Nazis" in Argentina was hardly "gratuitous" and wondered how someone who had been an "enthusiastic supporter of Hitler" could represent Argentina in the United Nations.[5] By August, the two countries had decided to declare the matter resolved. Official relations returned to the *status quo ante.* Matters, however, were not so easily solved for Argentina's Jewish community, which was subjected to a barrage of violent anti-Semitic attacks.[6]

In the United States, the story was the lead news item. CBS said the news had "electrified the world . . . as though Hitler himself had been found."[7] Some of the reaction, however, was negative. In the space of a month, *The Washington Post* ran two vituperative editorials condemning Israel's "jungle law" and predicting that an Israeli trial would be "tainted with lawlessness," "wreak vengeance," and "debase the law." The proceedings would be "divorced from justice." An Indiana paper branded Israel "a little upstart foreign state." *Time* condemned Israel's "high handed disregard of international law." *The New York Post* predicted that this would be a "show trial" which should rightfully be held in Germany. *The Christian Science Monitor,* taking an even more extreme stance, argued that Israel's claim to have the authority to adjudicate crimes against Jews committed outside of Israel was identical to the Nazis' claim on "the loyalty of persons of German birth or descent" wherever they lived.[8] Some of the more vituperative attacks came from William Buckley's *National Review.* He devoted three editorials to the topic within weeks of the capture. In surprising statement, Buckley described Eichmann as having had "a hand in exterminating *hundreds of thousands*" (emphasis added). Condemning the proposed trial as a "pernicious" effort designed to speak for a "mythical legal entity (the Jewish People)," Buckley marveled that it was to last three months, whereas the Christian Church's focus "on the crucifixion of Jesus Christ [lasts] for only one week of the year." This, he declared, was symptomatic of the Jewish "refusal to forgive." Buckley saw in the trial the "advancement of Communist aims" and the fanning of the "fire of anti-Germanism." (In later years, Buckley spoke with an exceptionally different voice. In a stunning forty-thousand-word essay titled *In Search of Anti-Semitism*, he admitted to his father's overt anti-Semitism and concluded that the writings of two conservative commentators and long-term contributors to the *National Review*, Joe Sobran and Pat Buchanan, were anti-Semitic.[9]) The criticism grew so intense that Amos Elon, *Haaretz*'s New York correspondent, mused: "The world . . . did not think like we did. . . . What appears to us to be 'historic justice' looks to others like a semi-pathological legacy of a traumatic experience." However, even the more severe critics made some grudging concessions about Israel's action. *The Washington Post* declared it "far wide of the mark" to attribute Israel's commitment to trying Eichmann to "animal vengeance." It came from a "mighty spiritual yearning for some measure of redress." *The New York Times*, which condemned Israel's actions as "immoral" and "illegal," conceded that Eichmann's trial would be fair because "Israeli courts yield to no one in the probity of their judges or the objectivity of their justice."[10]

The critics of Israel's actions did not just focus on the kidnapping. Some argued that because the law under which

Eichmann would be tried was passed in 1950 the trial constituted retroactive justice. Others questioned whether Jewish
judges could be impartial when the defendant was a Nazi
criminal. They failed to note that Nuremberg had also relied
on what could be considered retroactive justice—that is,
crimes against humanity. The concept of crimes against
humanity had been discussed in the international arena
early in the twentieth century and in relation to Turkey's
actions against the Armenians. Only at Nuremberg, however, was the notion of such crimes established as positive
international law. The critics who questioned the impartiality of Israeli judges also failed to note that the Poles conducted war-crimes trials after the end of the war and few
people had questioned whether their judges could be impartial, despite the fact that the Poles had been victims. Even
the solutions critics offered—that the trial should be held in
Germany or before an international tribunal—did not take
account of basic realities. There *was* no international body
to try him. The World Court adjudicated cases between
nations, not against individuals. The Nuremberg tribunals
could be reconstituted to hear successor cases, but, given
Cold War realities, that was a far-fetched possibility. There
was no groundswell of West German support for holding the
trial there. Many of the major German press outlets were
quite content to see it held in Israel. The *Frankfurter Allge-
meine* Zeitung observed, "It is not for us to question the
Israelis as to the where and how of the arrest. . . . It is of no
importance *where* Eichmann is brought to justice." The *Neue
Ruhr Zeitung* declared Israel "legitimized to try Eichmann."

The *Frankfurter Rundschau* found "any legal basis acceptable" as long as it "guarantees an orderly trial."[11] Chancellor Adenauer feared that a trial in Germany would highlight that the German government was riddled with former Nazi officials. In fact, his closest security adviser and the head of the Federal Chancellery was Hans Globke, who in 1935 had authored the legal commentary on the infamous Nuremberg Laws. Globke had determined the application of these laws, which stripped Jews of their citizenship, forbade marriages between Jews and "Aryans," and banned Jews from employing Aryan women in their homes (to protect them from being molested). Globke also had a hand in a 1938 rule that Jews must add the names "Israel" or "Sara" to their given names. The law exempted Jews with blatantly Jewish names from this regulation. Globke compiled the list of exempted names. One imagines him deliberating which names were "Jewish enough" so that adding "Israel" and "Sara" was superfluous. Globke was not the only former Reich official in an important position in postwar Germany. In the early 1950s, most of the leading positions in the Foreign Office were occupied by officials who had served the Third Reich. In 1952, Adenauer, reluctant to sweep them out, told the Bundestag, "I think we now need to finish with this sniffing out of Nazis." Adenauer found an unlikely ally in his efforts to keep Germany out of the picture. David Ben-Gurion, eager to forge ties between the two countries, wanted to convince Israelis that there was "one Germany before the Nazis" and "another after the Nazis." Consequently, as the trial drew near, he asked the prosecutor to make sure that his references to Germany were to *Nazi* Germany and to avoid mention of people such as Globke.[12]

As the debate about the capture and proposed trial of Eichmann intensified, much of the attention was focused, not surprisingly, on the man who made the decision— without consulting anyone else—that Eichmann should be pursued, captured, brought to Israel, and tried. The common "wisdom" is that Ben-Gurion orchestrated the capture and trial as a means of educating Israeli youth about the Holocaust. As with so many wisdoms, this is not supported by the facts. Hanna Yablonka, who has studied Israeli's reaction to the capture and the trial, has shown that he did not adopt education as a goal until well after Eichmann had been captured and was in Israel's hands. When he met with the editors of *Maariv* shortly after the capture, one asked if there had been any "outstanding events this year." Ben-Gurion replied, "I know of no outstanding events." When a journalist present mentioned Eichmann, Ben-Gurion insisted twice that the Eichmann matter was important only from a "journalistic standpoint." However, over the course of the year, his attitude would change. A year later, when the trial was under way, in his Independence Day address, he posited that the trial and the discovery of the Dead Sea Scrolls were the major events of the year, and that they both affirmed the historical legitimacy and necessity for a Jewish state. He had shifted his view in response to the importance the Israeli public accorded the capture and trial.[13]

Ben-Gurion's sense of the importance of the trial evolved, but his hostility toward those who criticized Israel's action was intense from the outset. The more outspoken the critics, the more Ben-Gurion bristled. In a lengthy interview, he told the *New York Times* that since the victims had been singled out *because* they were Jews the *Jewish* state was the proper entity to render justice. Had French citizens been killed because they were French, no one would question France's right to act. Ben-Gurion also contended that a trial would demonstrate that no longer could Jews be attacked with impunity. Now there was a Jewish state which would come to their aid. In the space of a few paragraphs, he twice described Jews who questioned Israel's right to try Eichmann as having an "inferiority complex." Ben-Gurion also believed that the trial would convey a contemporary political message. He considered those Arabs who threatened to destroy Israel and drive its inhabitants into the sea to be the Nazis' heirs. The Holocaust demonstrated, Ben-Gurion insisted, that such rhetoric could not be dismissed as hyperbole. *The New York Times* received an avalanche of letters about the interview. They ranged from describing Israel as a "vicious monster of a nation" to arguing that, since only Israel had cared whether he was captured, it was disingenuous for critics now to complain that he should be tried elsewhere. *Time* magazine described Ben-Gurion's contention that Israel was "the only sovereign authority in Jewry" that could apprehend any criminal who committed offenses against the Jews as "inverse racism."[14]

By the 1960s, the number of Jews and Jewish organizations in the Diaspora who thought that the existence of a Jewish state would compromise their own status as citizens of the countries in which they lived had diminished markedly. In the intervening years since the creation of the state, they had grasped that the existence of Israel did not threaten their political status. Nonetheless, some Diaspora Jews were still sensitive to any Israeli actions that might suggest to non-Jews that Israel was acting or speaking on behalf of Jews who were not its citizens. Eichmann's capture and, even more so, Ben-Gurion's comments to *The New York Times* left them uneasy. Not surprisingly, some of the most vituperative criticism came from Jews who had found a comfortable home in the highest reaches of the non-Jewish world. Harvard professor Oscar Handlin was an expert on immigration who had written a book on Jews in America—a topic not generally addressed by Harvard faculty in the 1950s. In a speech at Harvard and in subsequent articles, he lashed out at Israel's actions, denigrating the forthcoming trial as an "act of revenge in satisfaction of the private offense." Ignoring the fact that Eichmann had escaped from a POW camp, entered Argentina under an alias, and lived clandestinely in the country, he accused Israel of violating Eichmann's "right of refuge" with its "underhand[ed] kidnapping." For over a century, Handlin contended, Western liberal societies had opposed pogroms and attacks on Jews because they believed Jews shared with them "a common stake in human decency." This principle, which animated Jewish life in the West, was threatened by the kidnapping. There were certainly legal problems associated with Israel's kidnapping, but Handlin's juxtaposition of Eichmann's "right of refuge" with Israel's "underhand[ed]" actions and description of the Holocaust as a "private offense" are astonishing. More stupefying, however, is that, but fifteen years after millions of Jews had been murdered when most Western nations had barred them entry, he waxed rhapsodic about the West's conviction that it shared with Jews a "common stake in human decency." Handlin seemed oblivious that during the war, as Saul Friedländer has observed, "not one social group, not one religious community, no scholarly institution or professional association in Germany and throughout Europe declared its solidarity with the Jews." Predictably, Rabbi Elmer Berger, the leader of the anti-Zionist American Council for Judaism, described the trial as a "Zionist declaration of war" against American Jews' claim to equal citizenship. Psychologist and anti-Zionist Erich Fromm, writing in the anti-Zionist *Jewish Newsletter*, seemed to have lost any sense of perspective when he claimed that Israel's action was an "act of lawlessness of exactly the type of which the Nazis themselves . . . have been guilty."[15]

These anti-Zionist reactions were predictable. The reactions by some Zionists were less so. Nahum Goldmann, the president of the World Zionist Organization, suggested that an Israeli chief judge preside but that foreign jurists serve on the tribunal. Ben-Gurion considered Goldmann's critique a public slap at Israel's sovereignty and its judges' impartiality. Leveling the criticism the prime minister so often used when Jews questioned Israel's actions, he accused Goldmann of having "an inferiority complex." One must place this particular spat within its context. These men, both with oversized egos, had long sparred with each other. Ben-Gurion considered Goldmann a hypocrite for leading a Zionist organization but not settling in Israel. Goldmann resented Ben-Gurion's attempt as prime minister of Israel to speak for all the Jewish people.

Even more troublesome for Ben-Gurion was the response of certain American Jews. He knew he could depend on American Zionists to support any decision he made. The group he had to woo was the American Jewish Committee (AJC). Ben-Gurion believed the AJC, with its wealthy, establishment members, was best positioned to influence American foreign policy. Though not a Zionist organization, it considered Israel a Jewish cultural, historical, and spiritual entity. It had become a proponent of a Jewish state during World War II, when it saw Jews abandoned to their fate. Nonetheless the AJC remained wary about any action on Israel's part that might raise doubts about Jews' loyalty to America. In 1948, when AJC leaders saw a proposed draft of the Israeli declaration of independence, they urged that references to "the Jewish State" be replaced by "the State of Israel." (They were not replaced.) In 1950, AJC president Jacob Blaustein, in an effort to assuage growing tensions between AJC leaders and the new state, flew to Israel to meet Ben-Gurion. In an exchange of letters, they agreed that "the people of Israel have no desire and no intention to interfere in any way in the internal affairs of Jewish communities abroad," and that the Israeli government would not in any way "undermine the sense of security and stability of American Jewry." Despite this agreement, differences continued to percolate. They had surfaced a few months before

Eichmann's capture, during a rash of anti-Semitic incidents in Europe and the Americas. Israel's Foreign Ministry sent notes to its counterparts, including the United States State Department, describing itself as "sensitive and alert to anything that affects our brethren." The AJC condemned this as interference in American Jews' domestic matters. They pointedly informed Israel that they felt entirely capable of handling this issue without its intervention. But this was not the only development that troubled AJC leaders. In March 1960, General Moshe Dayan had stated in a speech in Canada that Israel represented the rights of "all Jews." A few weeks thereafter, Golda Meir told a delegation of the Anglo-Jewish Association that Israel would "continue to speak for Jewry."[16]

Now, with Ben-Gurion justifying Israel's right to try Eichmann because it was the *Jewish* state, the question "Who speaks for the Jewish people?" assumed newfound relevance. With a trial in the offing, this debate might well be played out on an international stage, something Diaspora Jewish leaders feared greatly. Joseph Proskauer, a former AJC president, sent Ben-Gurion a private letter articulating these concerns. He urged Ben-Gurion to turn Eichmann over to Germany or an international tribunal. Ben-Gurion responded by drawing a direct line between the Holocaust and the State of Israel. Acknowledging that while Israel could not speak in the name of all Jews, he argued that it must speak for the victims of the Holocaust because they believed "with every fiber of their being that they belonged to a Jewish people." In truth, many of the victims believed no such thing. For Ben-Gurion, however, this was utterly immaterial. To buttress his argument, Proskauer had sent Ben-Gurion *The Washington Post* editorial that attacked Israel's claim that it could "act in the name of some imaginary Jewish ethnic identity." Ben-Gurion knew that the paper's former owner, Eugene Meyer, had been an ardent anti-Zionist. His daughter, Katharine, was unaware that her father was Jewish until her classmates at Vassar asked her about having "Jewish blood." Who, Ben-Gurion wondered, gave the *Post* the authority to determine whether there was a Jewish ethnic identity?[17]

As part of their continuing effort to stop Israel from holding the trial, AJC leaders met with Golda Meir to inform her that they had "arrived at a consensus" that the trial should not be in Israel. Though they did not doubt that Eichmann would get a fair trial, they feared that an Israeli trial would obscure the fact that Nazism was the enemy of mankind, and that Eichmann had committed "unspeakable crimes against humanity, not only against Jews." This objection was sure to win no sympathy from Ben-Gurion, Meir, or other Israeli leaders. Meir dismissed their objections by recalling the world's indifference to Jewish suffering during the Holocaust and its lack of interest in finding the criminals afterward. Still hoping to effect a change in Israel's plans, the AJC convened a group of prominent judges and lawyers. They suggested that Israel conduct the investigation and then hand Eichmann and any evidence it had gathered to an international tribunal. Israel summarily rejected this idea.[18] As the complaints mounted, Ben-Gurion's patience—never his strong suit—grew short, as was evidenced in an interview he gave to E. A. Bayne of the American Universities Field Staff. Bayne suggested that it might be best if Eichmann was not tried in Israel. Ben-Gurion exploded: "You think that we should not try Eichmann? You are a Jew? An American Jew?" When Bayne indicated he was not, Ben-Gurion continued: "I thought only an American Jew would question our right to try Eichmann. . . ."[19]

A few months later, AJC leaders, aware that they had lost the battle over the trial's venue, tried to get Israeli officials at least to reformulate their statements about the Final Solution. They traveled to Jerusalem, where they told government leaders that Israel's public comments about the trial should stress that not only Jews but also Germans had suffered severely because of Eichmann and the Nazis' actions. The AJC leaders also suggested that Israel cast its comments about the Holocaust in universal terms. The Americans explained that when synagogues were bombed they spoke to the press in "broader terms" and referred to them as "houses of worship" in order to overcome non-Jews' indifference. Israel should do the same and stop "harping constantly on the identity of the deceased Jews."[20] One can imagine Ben-Gurion's reaction. These Jews trumpeted their complete acceptance into American society, but when their synagogues were bombed precisely *because* they were Jewish institutions, they fell back on the generic "houses of worship" and avoided identifying the victims as Jews. In fact, one need not imagine Ben-Gurion's reaction. He expressed it quite explicitly at the meeting of the World Zionist Congress. Ben-Gurion, still bristling at the American Jewish leaders' suggestions that he downplay *Jewish* suffering during the Final Solution, declared that the "Judaism of Jews of the United States is losing all meaning and only a blind man can fail to see the day of its extinction." Jews living outside of Israel faced "the kiss of death and the slow . . . decline into the abyss of assimilation." All Jews, he announced, belonged in Israel. As a result of his comments, the already shaky relations between Israel and American non-Zionists almost imploded. The AJC immediately charged him with violating the Blaustein understanding. Eventually, in an attempt to keep relations from completely disintegrating, Blaustein met with Ben-Gurion and convinced him to offer "strong official reaffirmation" of their agreement that Israel did not see itself as speaking for or acting on behalf of all Jews.[21]

Long before the court was called to order, it was evident that, in addition to Adolf Eichmann's crimes, many other issues would be in the docket.

3

Israel needed to consider far more than the anxieties of American Jews in preparing the trial. There remained essential practical issues that needed to be resolved. Who would judge, prosecute, and defend Eichmann? These constituted far more than just administrative hurdles. Given the extensive critique of its actions, Israel had to demonstrate that it could guarantee Eichmann a fair hearing.

Gideon Hausner, an accomplished commercial lawyer with no expertise in criminal law or courtroom procedure, had recently become attorney general. Though many Israelis hoped he would appoint an experienced prosecutor, he insisted on taking the job. Finding a defense attorney was far trickier. Unless Eichmann had good legal representation, Israel could not affirm that this trial was just. Yet could an Israeli defend a man who had a distinct role in the murder of millions of his fellow Jews? Many Israeli lawyers thought they could not. It would be wrong, one Israeli observed, to appoint an attorney who preferred to be prosecutor. But some Israeli lawyers, in the interests of ensuring that the accused received a fair hearing, volunteered to take the task. Officials at the Ministry of Justice feared that Israeli lawyers who defended Eichmann would be placing themselves in danger. Israeli officials worried that someone, particularly a person who had lost family members, might find it exceptionally difficult to differentiate between the accused and the person defending him. Foreign lawyers also volunteered. Most, however, were either neo-Nazis, incompetent, or both. Matters seemed to be at a standstill until the Eichmann family recommended Robert Servatius, who had been a defense attorney at Nuremberg but had never joined the Nazi Party. Servatius was not a member of the Israeli bar and could not therefore participate in a legal proceeding. The Knesset resolved this by passing a law authorizing a lawyer who was not a member of the Israeli bar to participate in a capital trial. Then the Eichmann family claimed it could not afford Servatius's fee, which was the equivalent of thirty thousand dollars. Generally West Germany paid the defense costs of its citizens who were tried for war crimes in foreign courts. This time it refused, ostensibly because Eichmann had fled Germany and hidden from prosecution. By so doing, Germany reasoned, he had renounced his right to call upon the country for assistance. In all likelihood, it also refused because it was anxious to keep this defendant at the longest arm's length possible. A German subvention of Eichmann's legal costs might have suggested that his homeland supported him. Facing an impasse, Israel agreed to pay Servatius's fees.

That left the choice of the judicial tribunal to preside over the trial. According to Israeli law, the selection of judges should have been in the hands of Benjamin Halevi, the president of the Jerusalem district court, since that was where the trial would be held. Halevi, however, had presided in 1954 at the trial of Israel Kasztner, the Hungarian Jew who had negotiated with Eichmann to exchange Jews for trucks. This 1944 negotiation, known as "blood for goods," resulted in the release of a trainful of seventeen hundred Jews. Some of its passengers were Kasztner's relatives or wealthy Jews who had paid handsomely to secure a place on the train. Others were orphans, Satmar Hasidim, or people chosen by Hungarian authorities. Kasztner had also managed to have a large group of Jews sent to a labor camp, rather than Auschwitz, thereby saving many of them. After the war, some Hungarian Jews condemned Kasztner as an opportunist who had saved his family and lived a privileged life under the Nazis, but failed to alert Hungarian Jews to their fate. They charged that he knew what awaited those who boarded the trains to Auschwitz. Others, particularly those who had been on the Kasztner train, considered him a hero who *had* tried to alert Hungarian Jews and who managed to save more Jews than anyone else, including the much-lauded Oskar Schindler. After the war, he came to Israel, affiliated with the leading political party, Mapai, served as a government spokesman, and lived a relatively modest life. Then an elderly eccentric pamphleteer set his sights on him. Malchiel Gruenwald, a Hungarian Jew who immigrated to Palestine in 1938, regularly issued mimeographed diatribes attacking Israeli leaders, primarily those associated with Ben-Gurion and Mapai. In one of these sheets he described Kasztner as the "vicarious murderer" of five hundred thousand Hungarian Jews, including the fifty-eight members of his immediate family. He also condemned the Zionist leadership in the Yishuv, the pre-state Palestinian Jewish community, for failing to rescue Jews during the war. The government sued Gruenwald for libeling one of its employees. Gruenwald hired Shmuel Tamir, who during that period had been a member of the Irgun, Menachem Begin's resistance group. Ben-Gurion and Begin were and remained arch enemies. Despite the fact that Gruenwald was the defendant, Tamir deftly turned the tables by claiming that Kasztner and the Jewish Councils, which were created by the Nazis to administer Jewish life in the ghettos, were guilty of collaboration. He also attacked Ben-Gurion and his associates who constituted the Zionist leadership in Palestine, accusing them of failing to rescue Hungarian Jewry. It became not a libel trial, but a trial of the victims. Rather than explicate what had happened during the Holocaust and give the public a sense of the overwhelming odds Jews had faced, the trial and Halevi's judgment were condemnations of the victims, or at least one segment of them, for failing to save their fellow Jews. In essence, it reinforced a long-standing Israeli perception that Holocaust survivors had done something untoward in order to preserve their lives. Judge Halevi promoted that view when his judgment exonerated Gruenwald and declared that Kasztner, by negotiating with Eichmann, had "sold his soul to the devil." Halevi's decision was eventually reversed by the Supreme Court, but not before Kasztner was assassinated outside his Tel Aviv home.

The possibility that the presiding judge in Eichmann's trial would be someone who had already declared him *Satan* worried many people. The proceedings might appear to be tainted from the outset. Many jurists and politicians, including the chief justice of the High Court of Justice, implored Halevi to step aside. Halevi refused, on the grounds that the opposition against him was rooted not in his statements about Eichmann, but in the government leaders' fears that he might allow the trial to become a forum for renewed criticism of their behavior during the war.[1] Once again the Knesset stepped in with a compromise law that stipulated that in capital cases a High Court judge should preside. That judge would be joined by two district-court judges, both of whom would be appointed by the president of the district court in which the trial was to be held. This allowed Halevi to participate but not to preside. High Court Judge Moshe Landau was named presiding judge. Halevi named himself and Judge Yitzhak Raveh as the two other members of the tribunal. All three were German Jews who had received their law degrees in Europe prior to immigrating to Palestine. Despite the controversy surrounding their appointment, they would win almost universal acclaim, even from the trial's severest critics.

Finally, there was the venue. Jerusalem's courtrooms were small, shabby, and not equipped with press quarters. Teddy Kollek, head of Ben-Gurion's office, was charged with finding an appropriate place for a trial that was sure to attract an international audience. He selected Beit Ha'am, a cultural center under construction whose name meant, appropriately enough, "House of the People." Its theater was transformed into a courtroom, replete with a glass booth for the defendant and compartments for hidden television cameras. Miraculously, its construction was completed in time.

Meanwhile, another drama was occurring near Haifa in Yagur Prison. This large complex had become a holding place for one man. Elaborate arrangements had been made to prevent Eichmann from harming himself, and others from harming him. One guard was assigned to watch him. Another guard watched the first guard, and a third watched the second. For added security, none of the guards had lost relatives in the Holocaust or even spoke German. At the same time, a far more onerous job was being conducted by Bureau 06, a special police unit created to do the investigation upon which the indictment would be based. Relying on the few existing books on the Holocaust and a mound of documents, including the entire Nuremberg proceedings, they researched the Final Solution. In order to assemble the details of Eichmann's activities, they also requested pertinent documents from an array of European countries. Virtually all countries, including those behind the Iron Curtain, were forthcoming. The two exceptions were the USSR, which did not even reply to Israel's request, and Britain, which adamantly refused to release information on its part in the trucks-for-lives negotiations. Britain had played a direct role when it arrested Joel Brand, the Hungarian Jewish leader who had been negotiating with Eichmann. Eichmann dispatched him to the Middle East where he was to negotiate with the British. British officials, convinced that he was a German spy, arrested him.[2]

Bureau 06's chief inspector, Avner Less, a German Jew who had immigrated in 1938, at age twenty-two, was Eichmann's interrogator. He and his police colleagues anticipated that Eichmann might refuse to cooperate, something he was legally entitled to do. To their surprise, he spoke freely. He inundated them with details about the Final Solution. One morning he arrived with a written statement declaring himself "prepared, unreservedly, to say everything I know of events." He offered a confession of sorts: "I do not ask for mercy because I am not entitled to it. . . . I would even be prepared to hang myself in public as a deterrent example for anti-Semites of all the countries on earth." Despite this acknowledgment of his actions, he refused to acknowledge personal guilt. He told Less that he was just a "little cog" and "exclusively a carrier out of orders." He was not guilty, he insisted, because his superiors ordered him to do terrible things. Then, at Nuremberg, they implicated him in order to try to save themselves. If he was guilty of anything, it was of being too loyal. Bemoaning his fate, he complained that he was facing a trial while "those who planned, decided, directed, and ordered the thing have escaped responsibility."

Captain Less, who spent more time in direct exchange with Eichmann than practically anyone else, including possibly Eichmann's attorney, Servatius, had the same initial reaction to Eichmann as had the men who had grabbed him in Argentina. Instead of encountering "the sort of Nazi type you see in the movies: tall, blond, with piercing blue eyes and brutal features and. . . domineering arrogance," he found a "thin, balding man . . . [who] looked utterly ordinary" and who trembled incessantly during the early stages of the interrogation. Less surmised that Eichmann feared receiving the treatment he had meted out. One morning guards arrived to take him from the interrogation room. Anticipating that he was about to be shot—he was, in fact, being brought to a judge so his detention order could be renewed—his knees buckled and he cried out "in a pleading voice": "But Herr Hauptmann [Captain], I haven't told you everything yet." Less, however, soon discovered that this ordinary-looking man with nervous tics was capable of "cold sophistication and cunning." According to Israeli protocol, Less was supposed to interrogate, not cross-examine, Eichmann. Nonetheless, their exchanges often became an evidentiary duel. On those occasions, Less found Eichmann "sardonic, even aggressive." He would "lie until defeated by documentary proof." At that point, unable to claim he had not performed an incriminating act, he would insist that he had just been following orders. Less also discovered that, whenever Eichmann vigorously protested something was *not* true, it probably was. Eichmann, who endured this extended cross-examination without the benefit of legal counsel, was at a severe legal disadvantage. Less, on the other hand, had an entire police bureau and prosecutorial team backing him up. They carefully prepared the questions in order to elicit the most information from him and to catch any of his lies. This same imbalance would continue through the trial when

Servatius and one assistant, who was often in Europe interrogating witnesses, faced the prosecution's substantial legal team.[3]

Eichmann began by describing his "sunny" childhood to Less. Born in 1906 in the Rhineland to middle-class parents, he moved to Austria with his family, where his father had a less than successful career as an entrepreneur. His stepmother, a deeply religious woman, conducted daily family Bible readings. In one of those enduring historical ironies, Eichmann attended the same high school as Hitler, though Eichmann never spoke of the school's impact on him. Eichmann became friendly with a Jewish student and remained in contact with him even after he joined the Nazi Party. Probably hoping to convince Less he was not a dyed-in-the-wool anti-Semite, Eichmann boasted how they would stroll together in Linz despite the Nazi Party emblem he sported on his lapel. A lackluster student, Eichmann left school and took a series of dead-end jobs until he saw an employment notice from the Vacuum Oil Company. His stepmother had a relative, "Onkel Fritz," who, as a friend of "Herr Weiss," the owner, arranged for Eichmann to be interviewed for the job. At the interview he was told by Herr Popper, the senior executive conducting the interview, that normally he would be considered, at age twenty-two, too young for the job. Nonetheless, he was being hired "at the request" of Weiss. Both Weiss and Popper were Jewish. Onkel Fritz had Jewish relatives by marriage. As David Cesarani observes, this demonstrates how the Eichmann family did not allow any anti-Semitic sentiments it might harbor to prevent it from reaching out to Jews who could be helpful. Eichmann succeeded at his job. His responsibilities entailed ensuring the on-time shipping, transportation, and delivery of petroleum products. He supervised the building of gas stations where none had existed before. Eventually these organizational skills would stand him in very good stead.[4]

In 1932, while still working for Vacuum Oil, he joined the Nazi Party. His decision to join does not seem to have been motivated by a deep—or even a shallow—ideological position. In fact, it seems somewhat happenstance. Someone invited him to attend a Nazi Party meeting. While there, he was warmly greeted by Ernst Kaltenbrunner, a family acquaintance and a lawyer from a decidedly higher social class than Eichmann. Wearing a resplendent SS uniform, Kaltenbrunner declared, "You belong to us." Eichmann joined. Shortly thereafter, Kaltenbrunner gave him an SS membership form. He joined that as well.[5]

In 1933, he lost his job because of an economic downturn. Company policy was to terminate unmarried employees before terminating those who were married with children. He subsequently told his Nazi superiors that he had been fired because he was a party member—probably to win favor in their eyes by demonstrating the sacrifices he had made for the party. The problem with Eichmann's assertion, as Cesarani observes, is that he was not fired until a year *after* joining the party and was even given a generous severance package.[6] Ironically, at his trial the prosecution accepted at face value Eichmann's assertion that he had joined the party *despite* the jeopardy this posed to his job. It is unlikely that he joined in order to enhance his social and political stature. In 1932, the Austrian Nazi Party was a small, innocuous, often ridiculed organization. Eichmann was probably being honest when he told Less that he was attracted to the party because it offered an explanation for Germany's defeat in World War I as well as camaraderie and bonhomie. Though there is no evidence of his having been propelled to join *because* of anti-Semitism, it could hardly have been irrelevant. Anti-Semitism was rife in Austria, and few people were immune from it. For someone raised in this atmosphere, blaming Jews for Germany's problems made perfect sense. It fit snugly with so much of what they were hearing about Jews. Anti-Semitism may not have been in Austria's DNA, but it certainly was in the air the population breathed.

Initially, Eichmann was a weekend Nazi, disrupting the meetings of rival political parties, protecting Nazi gatherings, and engaging in street brawls with anyone who denigrated National Socialism. In short, he was a thug. In 1933, after Hitler became chancellor, the Austrian government began a crackdown on Nazis. Lacking employment and facing anti-Nazi government pressure, Eichmann left for Germany. There he received SS ideological indoctrination and military training, some of it quite grueling. He told Less how the concepts of "comradeship" and "solidarity" were impressed upon him during this period. In 1934, he applied to join the Sicherheitsdienst (SD), the SS's intelligence-gathering unit. Established in 1931 by Heinrich Himmler, and headed by Reinhard Heydrich, it was charged with the task of gathering intelligence on Germany's ideological and racial "foes." In 1934, it was an anemic group with a few hundred members. The notion that either the SD or Eichmann, who, unlike most other SD members, had little formal education, would play a decisive role in any major operation of the Third Reich, much less the Final Solution, would have seemed utterly far-fetched to a rational observer. Eichmann told Less that when he first joined the SD he thought he would be part of the team that protected Himmler. "One gets around; one sits in the car and merely has to keep a look-out." Given his SS training, this assertion is implausible.[7] Eichmann's first assignment was to alphabetize a card file of German Freemasons so that the SD could track them. He also worked at the SD's Freemason exhibit, where he arranged the display of regalia, seals, and organizational paraphernalia. It was mind-numbing work. In 1935, the SD created a desk to monitor Jewish organizations. Its director, Leopold Itz Elder von Mildenstein, encountered Eichmann during a visit to the exhibit and invited him to join the operation. Eichmann accepted happily. "I would have said yes to anything to get away from sticking those seals on."[8] Eichmann had to know, in light of both his ideological training and the anti-Semitic legislation issued during the first years of the Reich, that an SD department dedicated to the Jewish question would not be engaged in benign enterprises.

Mildenstein gave him a number of classic books on Zionism, including Herzl's vision for a Jewish state, *Der Judenstaat*, and asked him to write a report on the movement. His summary was published as an SS orientation booklet, which may have helped him win both a promotion to staff sergeant and appointment as head of the Zionist desk. His new assignment was to study the myriad of domestic and foreign Zionist organizations and to develop a network of spies that would inform on them. His first paper on Zionism combined the history of the movement, which he generally got right, with nonsensical racial and conspiratorial theory, most of which any reader whose worldview was not infused with anti-Semitism would have dismissed as phantasmagorical tripe. The latter included his charge that the Zionist defense unit, the Haganah, then a modest organization, had, under the leadership of France's premier, Léon Blum, a Jew, infiltrated an array of foreign intelligence operations, including those in Britain and France.

Eichmann did more than just decipher the various Zionist organizations. He also developed connections with the leadership of the German Zionist movement. During the early years of the Nazi regime, Zionist leaders thought they might be able to work with the Third Reich, strictly on Jewish emigration. The Zionists wanted Jews to settle in Palestine. The SD wanted them out of the Reich. In an attempt to further these efforts, Eichmann and his immediate superior, Herbert Hagen, won permission from the SS leadership to accept an invitation from Zionist activists to visit Palestine in order to devise plans to encourage Jewish emigration from the Reich. The trip's primary purpose was meetings with ethnic Germans in the region and with Zionist leaders. Eichmann, who had not traveled beyond Austria and Germany, came to envision a broader plan. He expected to enter into high-level negotiations with Arab "nobility" and "politicians like Emir Abdullah and the Mufti of Jerusalem." Eager to make the proper impression, Eichmann asked for funds to purchase "one light weight, light colored suit and one dark suit as well as a light overcoat." His request was rejected, and instead of receiving the new suits, he and Hagen got stern warnings not to speak of their SD connections while in the Middle East. Though Eichmann would spin many fables about his time in Palestine, they were complete fantasies. After a day in Haifa, the British expelled them to Egypt. However, they did not let their aborted visit inhibit them from finding a vast Zionist conspiracy. Their report, which was primarily authored by Hagen, attributed Palestine's poor economic situation to the absence of Aryans and the presence of Jews. In Germany, Jews made money by cheating Aryans. In Palestine, there were no Aryans, so Jews cheated one another.[9]

Shortly after returning to Germany, Eichmann participated in an SD day-long seminar on Jewish affairs. His presentation, "World Jewry: Its Political Activity and the Implications of the Activity on the Jews Residing in Germany," detailed a variety of Jewish conspiracies, including a plan supposedly hatched by the head of the venerated French Jewish educational organization, the Alliance Israélite Universelle, for the assassination of Hitler and Julius Streicher, publisher of the notoriously anti-Semitic paper *Der Stürmer.* A Dutch Jewish organization joined the supposed conspiracy and enlisted the aid of the multinational margarine factory, Unilever. Eichmann told his audience that the Haganah had an array of heavy weapons, including aircraft. In his talk, Eichmann diagrammed Jewish organizations' complex and entangled relationship. Rather than see the reality of Jewish organizational life, which was then—and remains today—an unwieldy conglomerate of groups that duplicate one another, Eichmann found a giant conspiracy. This conspiratorial *idée fixe* had its roots in centuries of anti-Semitic hatred that had been nurtured by the church and in more recent centuries had blossomed within an enlightened secular Europe. It could be seen in France's treatment of Alfred Dreyfus and in Germany's intellectual circles. Nazi leaders had made this notion a linchpin of their ideology. Eichmann, however, had wholeheartedly adopted it, adding depth and detail. He and his SD colleagues subjected the spectrum of Jewish organizations to this kind of fantasy analysis. Saul Friedländer has posited that since "the organized enemy they were fighting was nonexistent . . . their own enterprise had to create it *ex nihilo*." Yaacov Lozowick argues quite persuasively that Eichmann and his colleagues, all of whom saw Jewish conspiracies wherever they looked, undoubtedly qualify as anti-Semites. Though this may seem obvious, it would become a matter of debate in the wake of the trial. "Not only were they indoctrinated. They were indoctrinators."[10] Adolf Eichmann found a comfortable home in the SD.

There remained one major issue—probably the most important of them all—to be resolved before a trial could proceed. What would be the scope of the crimes with which Eichmann would be charged? Bureau 06, adhering to standard police operating procedures, prepared files on those aspects of the Holocaust with which Eichmann could be directly connected. If Eichmann could not be directly linked to an event or action, they did not include it. Their list of proposed witnesses consisted only of people who had personally encountered Eichmann. Hausner found this completely unsatisfactory, told them to expand their perspective on Eichmann's crimes, and turned for help elsewhere. In *Justice in Jerusalem*, he acknowledged Rachel Auerbach of Yad Vashem, Israel's official memorial to victims of the Holocaust, for "placing at our disposal her department's huge collection of [survivor] statements."[11] She did far more than that; she became one of his most important resources. In the Warsaw Ghetto, Auerbach had been part of Emanuel Ringelblum's Oyneg Shabes archival group, which documented and recorded all aspects of ghetto life. Her one-hundred-page interview with escapees from Treblinka, which was smuggled out of the ghetto, was critical in alerting the world to the destruction process.[12]

She believed that the trial promised a "unique opportunity" to demonstrate the "full extent and unique nature of the destruction of the Jews of Europe." Rather than a small criminal trial that focused specifically on Eichmann's wrongs, she conceived of—and Hausner fully shared her view—a "large historical one." She helped provide the historical framework Hausner used in structuring much of his prosecution. She stressed for Hausner that, although the Final Solution had unfolded differently in each country, there was also a "characteristic uniformity" in the way in which it was organized and carried out. This "support[ed] the supposition that one hand ruled over them." Though her conclusion that "one hand"—Eichmann's—ruled was incorrect, her ability to see both the nuances and systemic nature of the destruction process is noteworthy.

While Hausner may have come to this effort intent on shining the spotlight on the witnesses, he found the perfect partner in Auerbach. It was she who, in great measure, enabled him to find the witnesses. She shared his view that the survivors had the perfect right to be "irrelevant" regarding Eichmann's specific crimes. Their testimony did not have to directly relate to what he did but should help paint the broad picture of the entire destruction process. Some observers considered this evidence highly prejudicial, while others believe that it is what gave this trial its place in history. Auerbach not only prepared lists of possible witnesses, many of whom Hausner selected, but also accompanied those lists with "suggestions and quotations" from the testimonies themselves. Hausner wove many of these into his examinations. It was Auerbach who urged him to call witnesses who could testify about German efforts to erase the evidence. Long before Eichmann's capture, Auerbach had conducted research on Operation 1005, the large-scale secret campaign to destroy evidence of the Final Solution by digging up the mass graves, pulverizing the bodies in specially adapted cement-mixer apparatuses, and erasing all traces of the atrocities. She also found two people who had participated as slave laborers in this effort. Both testified. Despite her devotion to her fellow survivors, Auerbach recognized that just because they said they had seen something did not ensure its reliability. She observed that many of those who volunteered to testify were people who claimed to have "seen Eichmann" at places where he had never been or where "no one could have identified him in those days." There were also those she described as "morbid publicity seekers." However, she considered most of those who came forward to be "highly responsible people."[13]

The problem with Hausner and Auerbach's approach was that Eichmann did *not* play a role in all aspects of the Final Solution. Nonetheless, the indictment, which Hausner issued in early February, took exactly that approach. It charged Eichmann with the "implementation" of the Final Solution, committing acts of "extermination" on Jews in Poland at death camps, murdering Jews in the USSR with the Einsatzgruppen, imposing sterilization and abortions on Jews, forcing Jews to live in conditions that were "likely to bring about their physical destruction," creating the mechanism to plunder Jews' property, and causing the death of thousands of Jews in forced-labor camps, ghettos, and transit camps. He was also charged with dispatching tens of thousands of Gypsies to be murdered and of deporting, under conditions of "servitude, coercion, and terror," more than a half-million Polish non-Jews and multitudes of others. Though his crimes against non-Jewish victims were included, they were clearly ancillary items.[14] At Nuremberg, the murder of the Jews had been an example of crimes against humanity. Here it would be the centerpiece.

But there was another reason for Hausner's displeasure with the limited and more focused nature of the case as envisioned by Bureau 06. He wanted to paint a portrait "with as much detail as possible . . . [of] the gigantic human tragedy." But that picture had to be painted in a way that would superimpose "on a phantom a dimension of reality."[15] He wanted the trial to capture the imagination of Israelis, among others, and give them a personal sense of what had happened. In order to do this, he would rely on those who had witnessed the events. They would fill the historical canvas with their own stories and make the victims and their experiences the trial's focus. This decision on his part would be controversial from a jurisprudential perspective, and monumental from a historical perspective. The prosecution would call a series of witnesses who had no connection with Eichmann. Some legal experts considered their testimony highly prejudicial and legally irrelevant. Much of it was based on hearsay, if not outright gossip. Yet their presence would transform the trial from an important war-crimes trial into an event that would have enduring significance. It would give a voice to the victims that they had not had before and would compel the world to listen to the story of the Final Solution in a way that it never had before.

4

On April 11, 1961, shortly before 9 a.m., Adolf Eichmann was quietly ushered into the glass booth that had been constructed in the Beit Ha'am's theater *qua* courtroom. Nearly all those present, including Hausner, had the predictable reaction. Could this normal-looking man be responsible for the death of millions? Elie Wiesel, who was reporting for *The Jewish Daily Forward*, observed that the assembled journalists considered it remarkable that he looked no "different from other humans." *The New York Times* columnist C. L. Sulzberger strangely noted that Eichmann was "more 'Jewish looking,' according to conventional definitions, than the two sunburned Israeli guards" at his side. There was, however, little time to reflect on this, because shortly thereafter the judges entered. In what may have been an effort to telegraph the message that this was to be, first and foremost, a *legal* proceeding, Presiding Judge Moshe Landau made no introductory comments and began reading the indictment.

He read in Hebrew, the language in which the vast majority of the trial was conducted. Over the coming months additional languages, including German, Yiddish, Hungarian, and English would be used in the courtroom. Some witnesses insisted on speaking Hebrew, despite the

fact that it was not their native tongue, while others preferred the familiarity of Yiddish. Irrespective of the language that they spoke, their words would be translated into
Hebrew. On those occasions when the judges wanted to
ensure that Eichmann understood them precisely or wanted
to expedite matters, they addressed him in German, his and
their native tongue. The proceedings were simultaneously
translated into English, French, and German. Hannah
Arendt was mystified by the fact that while the French was
"excellent" and the English was "bearable," the German was
a "sheer comedy" and often "incomprehensible." Given that
Beit Ha'am is adjacent to the Jerusalem neighborhoods in
which there lived at the time an exceptionally high concentration of well-educated Yekkies (German Jews), it is baf-
fling that good translators could not be found.

But this was not the only language-related drama taking
place behind the scenes. Israeli authorities distributed daily
bulletins on the trial in English, French, and German. The
trial was being covered by numerous journalists from Yiddish newspapers who challenged the Israelis about this
arrangement. Why, they asked, could bulletins not be made
available in Yiddish, which was, they reminded Israeli officials, the language "of Eichmann's victims." (In fact, many
of his victims spoke other languages, but it was the language
spoken by more Holocaust victims than any other.) How
could Israel ignore them? In a clear expression of 1960s
Israel's contempt for the language that it considered the
epitome of "exile," authorities told the protestors that they
"ought to know Hebrew" and suggested that they translate

the other language bulletins into Yiddish. Ultimately, a condensed version of the bulletins was issued in Yiddish.[1]

Eichmann's lawyer, Servatius, immediately rose to challenge the proceedings. Servatius had also been critical of the Nuremberg tribunal, which he had described as a "regression to barbarism." Reiterating the arguments that had been voiced over the past eleven months, he contended that the court lacked jurisdiction, because these crimes were committed prior to Israel's existence, on foreign soil, and against people who had no connection to Israel. How, then, could this court claim jurisdiction? Even if the court did claim jurisdiction, which Servatius knew they certainly would, a number of elements rendered the proceedings inherently unfair if not illegal. First of all, Eichmann had been abducted. Furthermore, because of the 1950 law, colleagues from the SS whom Eichmann might wish to call as defense witnesses could not enter Israel without facing arrest. If a witness could not call upon those who might support his position, how, Servatius legitimately wondered, could the trial be fair? Finally, using an argument that was almost guaranteed not to sit well with the judges who would have to decide whether it was a fair objection, Servatius challenged the judges themselves. He argued that, as Jews, they were incapable of remaining impartial in a case that dealt with the Final Solution.

Hausner then began his rebuttal. Drawing on international legal principles as well as examples of American and British case law, he challenged each of Servatius's objections. The UN had stipulated that Eichmann should be tried.

Israel was, therefore, not doing anything contrary to the will of free nations. Besides, courts had consistently ruled that *how* an accused is brought before a court does not negate its right to try him. In fact, he continued, the abduction had no bearing on the case, because Eichmann had been in Argentina illegally. Regarding the issue of "retroactive justice," he observed, this trial was no more retroactive than the Nuremberg tribunals. He acknowledged that Eichmann was being tried under a law that had been crafted after the war, and that had "retroactive application." However, even without it, everyone recognized the Final Solution as morally and legally wrong. Servatius's complaint about the inability of Eichmann's witnesses to enter Israel, Hausner argued, could be resolved by deposing them abroad. In contrast to Servatius, who had submitted a long written brief and had, therefore, outlined his core arguments, Hausner spoke for two and a half days. Piling legal precedent on top of precedent, Hausner droned on, even though he had no doubt that the judges would reject Servatius's arguments no matter what he said. His intended audience extended far beyond the courtroom. He was addressing critics throughout the world who had questioned the trial's legality. This, he wanted to make clear, was not "jungle justice."[2]

Reporters who had come to witness the trial of a mass murderer grew restless, and retreated to the snack bar to follow the breaking news regarding Yuri Gagarin, whom the Soviets had just launched into orbit. Spectators dozed. The judges grew impatient. Israeli commentators were brutal: "Do we need to cite a case from Idaho to prove that we are entitled to try Eichmann?" Though reporters may have been frustrated, in certain circles Hausner's approach met with praise. In the London *Sunday Times* Professor Hugh Trevor-Roper, who had previously attacked Israel's decision to conduct the trial, noted that he "listened to those endless English and American precedents and . . . saw clearly that the Israeli Government . . . is resolved that the case against Eichmann shall rest . . . unmistakably on the established theory and practice of civilized states." *The New York Herald Tribune*'s S.L.A. Marshall declared, "We hear American voices speaking to the tribunal through Mr. Hausner with such weight that if there is lingering doubt about the proprieties of the trial then our quarrel is with our own lawgivers." Patrick O'Donovan, writing in *The Observer*, described these elaborate examinations of precedent as an "essential preliminary, without which the trial would be a waste of time and a disgrace." The Earl of Birkenhead, who covered the trial for *The Daily Telegraph*, admitted that he had come to Jerusalem skeptical that Eichmann could be "impartially tried," but after listening to Hausner's opening speech he was convinced that "far from being unfair . . . scrupulous justice is [being] observed." Edith Templeton of *The Washington Post*, which had savaged the notion of a fair trial in Israel, opined that the legal objections to the trial had "fallen by the wayside under the driving, painstaking, mountainously documented argumentation of prosecutor Hausner."[3]

Finally, on the fourth day after the court had first been called to order, the judges rejected Servatius's objections.

They acknowledged that, even though judges had human emotions, they "are required to subdue them for otherwise [they] will never be fit to consider a criminal charge which arouses feelings of revulsion." At last, the trial itself could begin. Landau asked Eichmann to rise and to indicate how he pled to the charges. Standing in his glass box Eichmann responded to each charge, "In the sense of the indictment, no." This was the response intoned at Nuremberg by Göring, Ribbentrop, and the other defendants. In essence, Eichmann was proclaiming that, despite having possibly committed a wrongdoing, he bore no guilt because he was following orders.[4]

Hausner then rose for his opening address. He had completed it a few days earlier, yet, on the previous evening, he'd added an introductory paragraph. It—not the multiple pages that followed—remains one of the most oft-quoted passages of the entire trial. Addressing the judges with a biblical appellation, he evoked Cain and Abel as well as Emile Zola's *cri de coeur* about the French army's anti-Semitic treatment of Captain Alfred Dreyfus.

As I stand here before you, *Shoftei Yisrael*, Judges of Israel, to lead the prosecution of Adolf Eichmann, I do not stand alone. With me in this place and at this hour, stand six million accusers. But they cannot rise to their feet and point an accusing finger towards the man who sits in the glass dock and cry: *"J'accuse."* For their ashes were piled up in the hills of Auschwitz and in the fields of Treblinka, or washed away by the rivers of

Poland; their graves are scattered over the length and breadth of Europe. Their blood cries out, but their voices are not heard. Therefore it falls to me to be their spokesman and to unfold in their name the awesome indictment.

Eichmann, he declared, was a link in the long chain of anti-Semites who wished to destroy the Jewish people. He was the scion of Pharaoh (Egypt), Haman (Shushan/Iran), and Chmielnicki (Poland), all of whom had the same objective for the people of Israel: "to destroy, to slay, and to cause to perish."[5]

From a distance of five decades, and after too many encounters with people who arrogate the right to speak in the victims' names, it is hard not to find this rhetoric historically glib and self-aggrandizing. Yet, if we read it in the context of 1961, it is evident why it left many people breathless. Now, for the first time, the Jewish people, who during the war had looked this way and that for someone to speak on their behalf, had risen, not to implore others to save them but to prosecute. Here was a representative of the Jewish people speaking, not as a supplicant begging for help, but as a government official demanding long-delayed justice. Most important, he was not addressing some foreign authority who might or might not deign to take the Jews' fate into consideration. He was speaking to *shoftei Yisrael*, representatives of a country that, had it then possessed the sovereignty it now had, would have done more than grant the victims refuge. Israel would have welcomed them home.

Some critics claim that Ben-Gurion manipulated the trial from behind the scenes. In fact, one of the few aspects of the trial into which he had direct input was Hausner's speech. Hausner had shared an earlier draft of his speech with Ben-Gurion. (Some critics contend that this was a breach of protocol. Others argue that Hausner represented the government, of which Ben-Gurion was the head.) Ben-Gurion's requests for changes had far more to do with history and politics than with forensics. Well aware of Adenauer's sensitivities, and anxious to do nothing that would frustrate Israel's attempts to develop closer relations with West Germany, Ben-Gurion asked Hausner to use the term "*Nazi* Germany" rather than "Germany," and to mention Hitler's name early in the speech, so as to leave no doubt that today's Germans were *not* those of the Third Reich. The prime minister did not have to tell Hausner to argue that the Holocaust was a link in the enduring chain of anti-Semitism. Hausner came to the job with that view.

Hannah Arendt dismissed his speech, particularly its opening, as "cheap rhetoric and bad history," but others were transfixed. *The New York Times* observed that Hausner, who had thus far been dry and pedantic, had opened on a "dramatic note," and that muffled sounds of sobbing echoed through the courtroom. Israeli writer Haim Gouri saw the lawyer who had tried everyone's patience with endless legal precedents transformed into a "great figure of lamentation." *The Washington Post* described Hausner's opening as a "mighty chronicle" that "held the packed courtroom in the grip of compulsive attention." There was "harrowing drama—but it was not staged. . . . It sprang solely from the power of overwhelming truth." Another observer found in Hausner's words the "eloquent thundering" of ancient prophets who "strode across the Judean Hills—perhaps on this very spot"—and engaged in a "fearless condemnation of iniquity."[6]

This praise for the speech notwithstanding, there is no doubt that Hausner got much of the history wrong. Depicting Eichmann as the Final Solution's chief operating officer, he held him responsible for every aspect of it, including shootings in the East, European deportations, ghettos, and death camps. Hausner's portrait of Eichmann reflected the prevailing historical consensus at this time. Historians tended to think of the Third Reich as a highly organized top-down bureaucracy, where power flowed from higher pinnacles in an easily identifiable and highly regulated fashion. In fact, as historians now recognize, the Third Reich was far more amorphous than that. Different agencies and people within the same agency competed for power and control. Ideas flowed in two or more directions, and even in relation to the Final Solution, subordinates often took the lead. Their actions were then subsequently authorized by those above them. Their actions were in synch with an ideology of Jew hatred which was nurtured by the Nazi leadership. The differences of opinion among the members of the hierarchy were not over whether to persecute the Jews but over how to do so. In contrast to Hausner's accusation, Eichmann did play a decisive role in aspects of the Final Solution, though he certainly did not control most aspects of it.

But even if Hausner got this wrong, some elements of his depiction of Eichmann were quite accurate. In every instance where his imprint was to be found—volunteering suggestions, giving orders, or interpreting policy— Eichmann always chose the most stringent option. Ordered to deport one trainload of Jews, he pushed for two. Ordered to end deportations on a certain date, he fought to extend the deadline. Ordered to deport Jews from one region, he included those from another. A portrait emerged of a man who was proactive, energetic, and a creative master of deception. This defendant, working with a group of subordinates who were dedicated to their task and to him, arranged the deportations of a great portion of European Jewry.

He pursued individual victims with the same zeal with which he deported multitudes—and sometimes even greater zeal. When the German Foreign Office interceded on behalf of a senior French officer who was a Jew, Eichmann unequivocally rejected its request on "principle." When the Swiss government tried to free some of its citizens, Eichmann refused: they knew too much. When the Italians learned that an Italian officer's widow was being held in Riga and asked for her release, Eichmann refused. When the Italians, including the Fascist Party representative, asked again, Eichmann rejected their request and, lest anyone overrule him, ordered her to be held at Riga. When the Italians asked the Germans to locate Bernardo Taubert, an Italian national who had been living in Lvov, Eichmann's deputy recommended that they be told to desist from such "superfluous requests." German authorities had "more important duties to carry out than to investigate the fate of a deported Jew."[7]

Now came the summoning of witnesses. Hausner had prepared a list of more than one hundred survivors, most of whom had no direct link to Eichmann. Most of them had probably never heard his name during the war. Hausner did not need their testimony to prove Eichmann guilty—the myriad of documents he planned to introduce would have sufficed. But the witnesses would tell the story in an unprecedentedly concentrated fashion. Some had told their stories before, to family, friends, and in public settings. But this time, rather than recollecting, they would be testifying, in the full meaning of the word. Both the retelling and the size and profile of those who would be listening would be entirely different. Never before had they told their stories in front of such a broad international audience. Reporters from Asia, South America, North America, and, of course, Europe packed the courtroom. Even if many reporters would leave after the opening to chase down the next big story—the Bay of Pigs invasion in Cuba began during the first week of the trial—never before had there been such consistently high level media coverage of this tragedy.

In addition to the witnesses, Hausner had another source, with the potential to be most damning of Eichmann. While in Buenos Aries, Eichmann had been cajoled by Willem Sassen, a Dutch-German member of the Waffen-SS, to co-write a history of the Final Solution that would present the "other" side of the story. Sassen, a forerunner of current Holocaust deniers, wanted to exonerate Hitler and lower the toll of those murdered. Eichmann, apparently desirous to clear his name and to earn some money, readily agreed. Though Eichmann found it fantastic that anyone could think the Final Solution could occur without Hitler's imprimatur, the Eichmann who emerged in the sixty-seven tapes and hundreds of pages of transcripts showed no remorse. He bemoaned the fact that the regime had not killed more Jews and expressed great satisfaction about how smoothly the deportation process had run. He declared that if the official Reich statistician had correctly concluded that "we killed 10.3 million, then I would be satisfied." But Hausner had a problem: he had the page transcripts, but could not access the original tapes. Servatius, knowing how damaging the transcripts could be to his client's case, objected to their use. But among the pages in Hausner's possession were those with Eichmann's handwritten corrections and edits of the tape transcripts. This would end up constituting some of the most incriminating evidence.[8]

Hausner began by calling Police Inspector Less, who had spent so many hours interrogating Eichmann. Less played tapes of his interrogation of Eichmann. The court heard Eichmann describe the preparations he witnessed for mass murder. Deep in a forest he had seen the building of an hermetically sealed structure designed to gas Jews. On another occasion he watched Jews being forced to undress and enter a truck to be gassed. On the tape Eichmann described the moment when the doors opened as "the most horrible thing that I had ever seen in my life." As civilians with pliers moved among them, pulling gold-filled teeth, the bodies seemed still to be "alive—their limbs were so supple." After witnessing a mass shooting in Łódź, he complained to his superior, Gestapo Chief Heinrich Müller. His concerns were not about the victims but about the shooters: "We were bringing up people to be sadists." He described visiting Auschwitz and Treblinka. At the latter camp he watched while a "line of naked Jews were entering a house . . . to be exterminated by gases." He recounted how Heydrich had told him that "the Führer had ordered the physical destruction of the Jews."[9] This was probably the most vivid and specific perpetrator-testimony about the murders that had thus far been heard in public.

Next, in an attempt to paint a portrait of the cultural world that had been destroyed, Hausner called the renowned historian Salo W. Baron of Columbia University. Baron provided a dizzying array of facts and figures about European Jewish life. However, rather than his scholarly discourse, it was a brief personal observation that most vividly captured the scope of the loss. After immigrating to the United States, he twice returned to visit his hometown, Tarnów, in Poland. In 1937, he found a population of twenty thousand Jews, "outstanding institutions, a synagogue that had existed there for about 600 years, and so on." When he returned in 1958, there were twenty Jews, of whom "only a few . . . were natives of Tarnów." This observation encapsulated the tragedy more profoundly than the hours of Baron's erudite scholarship.[10]

With the context in place, Hausner began to track Eichmann's career as a Jewish "specialist." After the March 1938

Anschluss, the German "invasion" of Austria, an action most Austrians welcomed enthusiastically, Eichmann's professional status began to rise rapidly. The Austrians, who have until recently claimed that they were the Third Reich's first victims, enthusiastically looted Jewish property and subjected Jews to multiple humiliations. Elated Viennese jeered as Austrian youth compelled Jews to scrub the street on their hands and knees. These anti-Semitic actions were so extreme that German officials called for order. They did not object to the humiliation and degradations. Rather, they objected to the ad hoc confiscation of Jewish property and the lack of order. About a week after the entry of German troops, Eichmann was dispatched to Vienna by the SD with instructions not to attack Jews physically, but to eject them from Austria. He immediately ordered all Jewish organizations to cease operating and had the communal leaders arrested. He then summoned a few of them to a meeting. Now, twenty-three years later, some of those same leaders took the stand in Jerusalem. Moritz Fleischmann described for the court how Eichmann, seated behind a large desk in his black SS uniform, compelled them to stand before him. After telling a completely fabricated story about being born in Palestine and speaking Yiddish and Hebrew fluently, he announced that he would "administer and direct" all Jewish matters and would "solve the Jewish problem in Austria completely." Austria would become *Judenrein* (Jew free). He demanded "unwavering obedience and unfailing cooperation and compliance with all his instructions and directives." If Eichmann intended to scare these Jews, he succeeded.

Fleischmann recalled the "alarm and . . . fear" Eichmann's activities aroused in Viennese Jewry. "We sensed it at once."[11]

In order to emigrate, Austrian Jews had to surmount a myriad of hurdles. Bills had to be paid, tax liens settled, and exit visas secured. Desperate Jews raced from office to office to obtain the requisite documents. At each step, officials tormented and taxed them. To rectify this situation, Jewish leaders proposed to Eichmann the creation of a Central Bureau for Emigration, which would bring together under one roof the entire emigration process. Eichmann tweaked their proposal slightly and sent it to his superiors in Berlin, passing it off as his initiative. It was approved, and soon, in a large hall in the Rothschild Palais, Jews were moving "seamlessly" through the process. Emigration rose markedly. Franz Meyer, a Berlin Jew who visited the operation, described it for the court. It was "most terrible, most terrible," like "a flour mill connected to some bakery. You put in at the one end a Jew who still has capital and has, let us say, a factory or a shop or an account in a bank, and he passes through the entire building from counter to counter, from office to office—he comes out at the other end, he has no money, he has no rights, only a passport in which is written: You must leave this country within two weeks: if you fail to do so, you will go to a concentration camp."[12] Eichmann's goal was not just to get rid of Jews, but to ensure that the Reich would not be left with those Jews too poor to emigrate. He instructed that financial aid being sent from abroad by Jewish organizations be used to support the emigration of poor Jews. This turned out to be a win/win situation for the Nazis. Over the next two years, the American Jewish Joint Distribution Committee alone sent two million dollars to Vienna. Eichmann exchanged this prized foreign currency at a rate that was highly favorable to the Germans and then used the funds to pay for the emigration of poor Jews.[13]

Eichmann reveled in his power. Not long after arriving in Vienna, he wrote a letter to an SS colleague boasting of his power over the Jewish leaders. Hausner entered the letter into evidence. Though twenty-two years had passed since he had written it, Eichmann's pleasure at the control he exerted over this august Jewish community was chilling. "I put these gentlemen on the double, believe me," the thirty-two-year-old high-school dropout gloated. "I have them completely in my hands, they dare not take a step without first consulting me. That is how it should be, because then better control is possible."[14] In Israel, of course, Eichmann put a radically different spin on his interaction with Jewish leaders. He cast it as a "decently businesslike" collaborative effort. It was so good that none of them, he insisted, "would have complained about me." A strikingly different picture was painted for the court by Aharon Lindenstrauss, who, along with Franz Meyer, was part of a delegation of German Jews the Gestapo sent to Vienna to observe the process. Eichmann's superiors, delighted that he was simultaneously getting rid of Jews and obtaining foreign currency, wanted these leaders to replicate the process in Berlin. Even before the delegation entered the Rothschild Palais, they were reminded of their status. Already using the language of dehumanizing objectification that would be fully realized during the Final Solution, the steel-helmeted SS guards outside the building phoned Eichmann's office to announce that *"Vier Stück aus Berlin sind angekommen"*—four "pieces" had arrived from Berlin. It was with Jewish leaders such as these four "pieces" that he claimed to have had a decent business-like relationship. Ushered past hundreds of Jews standing in the courtyard in the rain waiting to apply for passports, Lindenstrauss saw not "orderly emigration" but "deportation" pervaded by an aura of debasement and degradation. When the visitors arrived at Eichmann's office, a group of Viennese Jewish leaders were present. They reminded Lindenstrauss of "disciplined soldiers who stood to attention all the time and dared not utter a word. I had the impression that . . . they were afraid to move." The visitors were ushered into a large, beautiful hall, where Eichmann, sitting behind a desk, demanded that they move back to a distance of three to four meters. Once they were properly situated according to Eichmann's stipulations, Eichmann berated them for the slow emigration rate from the Altreich (pre-Anschluss Germany). One of the visitors, Dr. Hermann Stahl, blamed the slow pace on the emigration taxes, which left most Jews destitute. These moneys, he argued, should be used to finance emigration. Eichmann exploded: "Should we pay for keeping you old bags alive?" He warned the visitors to speed up the emigration, "otherwise you will certainly understand what fate awaits you."[15] Meyer had, as chair of the German Zionist organization, previously interacted with Eichmann. In his testimony he described for the court the marked difference between the man he knew from Berlin and the one he encountered in Vienna.

> I immediately said to my colleagues that I do not know whether I was meeting the same man. The change was so awful. . . . I previously had thought that this was a minor official, the type they call a "clerk" or a "bureaucrat" who fulfills duties, writes reports, and so on. Now, here was this man with the attitude of an autocrat controlling life and death, he received us impudently and crudely. [16]

When the delegation returned to Berlin, word of their experience spread. A reporter for a Yiddish-language French paper picked up the story and wrote an article in which members of the delegation described Eichmann as a *Bluthund* and *Judenfiend*, a bloodhound and an enemy of the Jews. An irate Eichmann summoned the leaders to Gestapo headquarters. Benno Cohn told the court how they stood behind a rope separating them from his desk while Eichmann subjected them to a barrage of "rude, barrack room language." When one of the leaders again complained that the Reich's taxation policy made it hard to get entry visas to other countries, Eichmann exploded, calling him an *alter Scheissack*, an old shit bag, and adding the ominous observation: "It seems it is a long time since you have been to a [concentration] camp."[17] Such was his decent relationship.

Jews were not alone in fearing Eichmann's newfound power. Bernhard Lösener, head of the Ministry of the Interior's Jewish Desk, visited the Viennese emigration operation. After the war, he recalled that he wanted to talk with the Jews there but decided against it because he "felt himself under Eichmann's surveillance." He witnessed how "women pulled their children aside in horror as soon as they saw Eichmann, who casually passed by as though along an empty street, shoving aside the waiting human unfortunates." Jewish leaders who had been waiting for hours "immediately jumped up. . . . Eichmann rapidly pointed each out by name, told me with equal rapidity which area they would report on; they then immediately droned through their information like trained animals. The expression of justifiable mortal fear could be read in each face." If a Nazi official felt personally afraid, one can imagine the terror Eichmann evoked in the Jews. Eichmann was soon boasting of having facilitated the emigration of fifty thousand Jews. Though this was an inflated figure, his superiors in Berlin credited him with designing a system that increased emigration, retained Jews' assets, and brought foreign currency into the Reich's coffers.[18] These skills would become even more prized by his superiors as the Final Solution entered its more dire stages.

With the start of the war in 1939, the number of Jews under German control increased exponentially. It did not take long for German officials to recognize that emigration was no longer a viable solution. Rather than push the Jews out of the Reich, their goal became finding some Reich controlled territory appropriate for resettling Jews. When Heydrich convened a meeting a few days after the beginning of the war to discuss moving the Jews to the farthest corner of

German-controlled territory, Eichmann was the most junior officer present, an indication that he was now considered a central player. Shortly thereafter, in October 1939, Eichmann was instructed to deport the Jews of Katowice, a Polish city destined to be incorporated into the Reich. Eichmann rushed to make the arrangements and, despite his relatively low SS rank, managed to have Jews from both Vienna and Ostrava, a town near Katowice, included among those to be deported. He raced from city to city to organize matters. It is telling that he left finding a destination to be the final step. Getting Jews out of the Reich was far more important than figuring out where they might go. Shortly before the trains were scheduled to roll, he flew to Poland. He had instructed that he was to be met by a Mercedes and a Lancia. They were to convey him and his party to a region "suitable" for depositing the Jews. He quickly decided on Nisko, a small wetland area conveniently located near a railroad. When the first group of Jews arrived, he was there.

Witness Max Burger told the court what the Nazi officer who greeted them—he later learned it was Eichmann—had said: "The Führer has promised the Jews a new homeland. There are no flats and no houses; if you carry out the construction you will have a roof over your head. There is no water. Wells in the whole area are infested; cholera, dysentery, and typhoid are rampant. If you start digging and find water, then you will have water." After walking a number of kilometers, they were told to leave their luggage and climb up to the site of the proposed settlement. Horse-drawn carts brought the luggage to the foot of the site. The horses were then released. The men were harnessed to the carts and instructed to pull them up the hill. Eventually, those who could not work or were considered too old—over forty—were driven off in the direction of Soviet territory.[19]

Complications soon arose. The army needed the trains that were being used to deport these Jews. Moreover, Hitler decided to conduct a far more massive transfer of ethnic Germans living in Polish territories back to the Reich. Since the two programs could not be conducted simultaneously, Eichmann was told to halt his operation. Having predicted "flawless execution," Eichmann fought to dispatch another series of transports to Nisko. Even after receiving a telegram from the Gestapo to stop, he continued, arguing that since the communiqué was not from his superior he could ignore it. When subsequently told to suspend the transports, he dispatched yet one more train, in order to maintain "prestige." The couple of thousand Jews remaining in Nisko were left without shelter or support. Some were chased by the SS toward the river that abutted the Soviet border. The survivors returned to their homes. They paid their own fare.

The program's failure did not impede Eichmann's career. These, the first organized transports of Jews to Poland, became the prototype for subsequent transfers of multitudes of European Jews. By the end of 1939 he had demonstrated that tens of thousands could be removed from their communities without their or their neighbors' opposition. The victims, plied with promises about the opportunities awaiting them, cooperated. Despite the failure at Nisko, his superiors must have been satisfied with Eichmann's performance. Shortly thereafter, he was named "special officer" for the "clearing of the Eastern provinces." Ultimately the section of the RSHA, the Reich's main security office, that he led would be responsible for coordinating the deportation of approximately one and a half million European Jews to killing centers.

Hausner next began to call those who had witnessed the murderous aspects of the Final Solution. He had sought people with a "good story," who could bring the tragedy alive.[20] Among his initial witnesses were two women who did exactly that. Ada Lichtmann was called to testify about the "small-scale" terror in Poland. Speaking in Yiddish, the language that evoked the voices of so many victims, she described how the Germans conducted a mass shooting, killing adults and children: "I saw everything." An equally harrowing scene was described by Rivka Yoselewska. She told the court how a German shooter debated whom to shoot first, her or the child she was holding. After the child was shot, she fell into the pit that already held the bodies of most of her family. Miraculously, she was later able to crawl out. When she did, she saw a fountain of blood spurting from the ground, an observation that evoked Eichmann's recollection in his interrogation of having also seen such a fountain.[21] Equally troubling was Professor Georges Wellers's description of the Jewish children in France who were rounded up in July 1942 and brought to Drancy, the camp outside of Paris, without their parents. They slept over a hundred to a room on "straw mattresses on the ground—mattresses which were filthy, disgusting, and full of vermin," many with no adult allowed nearby. It was not uncommon for them to awake during the night screaming for their parents. Some were too young to know their own names. Since they had already been interned in other camps, their state of cleanliness was "frightful." This was compounded by the waves of diarrhea that affected many of them. Wellers told of taking a fellow camp inmate, René Blum, brother of French premier Léon Blum, to see the children. They spoke with one boy who was "remarkably handsome, with a face which was very intelligent. . . . He wore clothes which must have been of very good quality, rather stylish, but in a pitiful condition. One foot was bare." When asked about his parents, the boy said, "My father goes to the office and Mummy plays the piano." They reassured him that he would soon rejoin his parents, though both Wellers and Blum knew the child was headed for Auschwitz. The boy happily showed them a biscuit he was saving for his mother. Blum "bent over the little boy who looked very happy, very engaging. He took his face in his hands and wanted to stroke his head, and at that moment the child, who only a moment ago had been so happy, burst into tears." The four thousand children, rounded up by the French police, were all deported to Auschwitz a few weeks later on Eichmann's orders. When the time came for that deportation, many of the children fought and had to be brought to the roundup place "struggling and screaming."[22]

Hausner elicited from each witness as many details as the

often impatient judges would allow. He also did something that stupefied many people. He did it not once but multiple times, in open court, and in front of a gallery filled with reporters and survivors. In Israel and many other places there was a persistent leitmotif when the discourse turned to Holocaust survivors: *Why didn't you resist? Why did you comply with the orders? There were fifteen thousand prisoners and a couple of hundred guards. Why didn't you revolt?* These questions were rarely addressed directly to survivors, certainly not in such a confrontational fashion or in such a public setting. Yet Hausner asked not once but multiple times. Ya'akov Gurfein told how his mother had pushed him from a deportation train. He managed to make his way to the Kraków Ghetto. When he realized how bad things were in the ghetto, he escaped to Plaszów, the labor camp on the edge of Kraków made famous by *Schindler's List*. He subsequently escaped from there and, after crossing Slovakia, Romania, and Hungary, reached Palestine. Hausner asked this remarkably resourceful man, "Why did you board the train?" Despite the passage of eighteen years, his answer captured both the despair and the inexplicable residue of hope that the victims had felt. "This was in 1943. After so many years we did not have the strength to resist any more. . . . We wanted to die more quickly." So why, Hausner persisted, did you jump? "The moment we saw that the train was going in the direction of Belzec . . . some spark was . . . kindled within people who wanted to save themselves."[23] Not long thereafter, Hausner asked again, this time of Magistrate Moshe Beisky. He was revered for having passed up opportunities to escape from Plaszów because he knew that the commander, Amon Göth, would apply collective punishment, probably death, to the eighty other prisoners in his barracks if he escaped. When he entered the witness box, the judges offered him the option of sitting while he gave testimony. He declined. For an hour, he stood and dispassionately described what he had witnessed. At one point, fifteen thousand prisoners were ordered by SS men armed with machine guns and bayonets to watch as a young boy was brought to be hanged. The child was lifted up to the gallows, but the rope broke. Beisky recalled, "He was again lifted on to a high chair which was placed under the rope." The child then "began to beg for mercy. An order was then given to hang him a second time." Beisky had just barely begun to describe this harrowing scene when Hausner pounced: "15,000 people stood there—and opposite them hundreds of guards. Why didn't you attack? Why didn't you revolt?" Beisky struggled to respond. The articulate witness was replaced by a man who floundered, groped for words, and left sentences unfinished: "This was already in the third year of the War. . . . Nevertheless there was still hope. Here were people working on forced labor, they apparently needed this work. Possibly, maybe . . ." Mid-sentence, he stopped and asked to sit. After a moment's pause, he gave voice both to the terrible dilemma Jews faced and to the obtuseness of the question.

> I cannot describe this . . . terror inspiring fear. . . . Nearby us there was a Polish camp. There were 1,000 Poles. . . . One hundred meters beyond the camp they

had a place to go to—their homes. I don't recall one instance of escape on the part of the Poles. But where could any of the Jews go? We were wearing clothes which . . . were dyed yellow with yellow stripes. [In] the hair at the centre of [our] head . . . they made a kind of swath in a stripe 4 centimeters in width. And at that moment, let us suppose that the 15,000 people within the camp even succeeded without armed strength . . . to go beyond the boundaries of the camp—where would they go? What could they do?[24]

After reading Beisky's unrehearsed answer, I photocopied it and slipped the page into the file folder I use for my weekly lectures in my Holocaust-history course. Someday—probably long before this manuscript appears as a book—a student will ask, "Why didn't they fight back?" And I will give her the spontaneous testimony Gideon Hausner elicited from a very brave, but at that moment rebroken man.

Why did Hausner ask this question? Was he using these interchanges to impress upon young Israelis the difference between the response of most Diaspora Jews to persecution and that of the "new" Israeli Jew? Hannah Arendt excoriated him for asking it. Echoing Beisky, she correctly observed that no one else—Jew or non-Jew—acted any differently. After his testimony, Beisky, shaken and angry at being blindsided, accosted Hausner. In his memoir Hausner recalled Beisky's angry question: "Why did you not at least warn me beforehand?" Hausner told Beisky he wanted a "spontaneous reaction." Though Hausner's tactics seem callous, he believed that the answer he elicited from Beisky justified them. He described Beisky's testimony as "the most convincing piece of human truth I have ever heard on the subject." Critics interpreted his question as emanating from the self-assured, if not arrogant, perspective of the person who was not there but who nonetheless knew what he would do. Hausner's objective was in fact quite the opposite. He wanted to demonstrate the inherent unfairness of this question. Over the course of his preparation for the trial, he had come to know the survivors. Shortly before the trial, he told the Israeli Cabinet that he would resist letting the courtroom become a venue for "clarifying how the victims should have resisted." He criticized Judge Halevi for letting that happen at the Kasztner trial. "It is very easy to sit on the court . . . and say Kasztner ought to have behaved in this way or that in Budapest in 1944." Hausner was well aware that native Israelis, who had vanquished five armies in 1948, did not comprehend why Jews who so vastly outnumbered their captors did not do the same. Hausner wanted them to understand why the two situations could not be compared. That is why he described Beisky's response as having "brought the trial to a new moral peak." The real wonder, Hausner observed after the trial, was that there *had* been so much organized and widespread resistance.[25]

A few days later, the resistance fighters, those to whom this question did not have to be asked, testified. On that day Kol Yisrael, Israel's radio station, which had halted its continuous broadcasts of the trial, resumed them. Now, many Israelis anticipated, would come respite from the unrelenting stories of victimhood. Yet these witnesses also spoke of suffering and humiliation. Yitzhak Zuckerman, who had been in the Warsaw Ghetto, could hardly contain his emotions when he described learning of the mass murder in Ponary Forest, outside of Vilna. "I left my parents and my family in Vilna. . . . As a child, I played nut games in Ponary. And here . . . they were putting to death Jews of Vilna in Ponary." His wife, ghetto fighter Zivia Lubetkin-Zuckerman, described the "fear of being collectively responsible for the acts of each individual Jew." Fifty Jews might be shot if one Jew resisted. She recalled the "strong young" German guards and the "cruelty" they directed "against helpless people." But then she added something that expanded the traditional concept of heroism. Initially, Jews in the ghetto thought that the Germans' objective was to "degrade . . . depress . . . starve us." By closing all educational institutions they would "change us into a nation of slaves, ignorant people, lacking culture." At that point, they decided to "develop a spirit of revolt." But the revolt of which she spoke was not the subsequent battle that would become an iconic element of the history of the Holocaust. "When I say 'revolt' I do not refer . . . to a particular rebellion but rather to preserve the human, social, and cultural character of the youth."[26] She, who fought with arms, insisted that heroism came in many forms. This was something young Israelis—and so many others—needed to hear.

Shortly thereafter, the leader of the Vilna resistance fighters, Abba Kovner, testified. In December 1941, he had called for active resistance against the Nazis. This was probably the first such call in all of Europe. In it, he used a phrase that subsequently was used colloquially as a means of denigrating the victims: "Let us not go like sheep to the slaughter." After leading the Vilna uprising, he joined a Soviet resistance group. He subsequently became a kibbutznik and one of Israel's leading poets. As a man of the land, arms, *and* letters, he epitomized the "new Jew." Yet his testimony was riddled with pain. He told of his student Tsherna Morgenstern, a "tall upstanding girl" with "wonderful eyes," who was taken with her classmates to Ponary. An SS officer ordered her to step forward: "Don't you want to live—you are so beautiful. . . . It would be a pity to bury such beauty in the ground. Walk, but don't look backwards." As she walked away, her classmates watched with envy until the officer shot her in the back. Kovner told all this and more. Toward the end of his speech—it was more that than anything resembling testimony—he turned to the judges and declared, "A question is hanging over us here in this courtroom: How was it that they did not revolt?" As a "fighting Jew," he would "protest with all my strength" if someone asked that question with even "a vestige of accusation." In fact, rather than question why most Jews did not rise up, people should recognize that not resisting was the rational thing to do. Resistance organizations are created by calls from a "national authority." There was no Jewish authority to issue that call. There was no one to organize an uprising. Rather than demean the victims, contemporary generations should recognize how "astonishing" it was that "there was a revolt. That is what was not rational."[27] Kovner's words, together with Beisky's earlier testimony, constitute eloquent responses to a question that people who live privileged and secure lives seemed to have few compunctions about asking.

Kovner had barely left the witness box when there was an unexpected turn of events. Judge Landau turned to Hausner and attacked not just Kovner's testimony but the entire premise of Hausner's prosecutorial strategy. With undisguised fury, Landau lectured Hausner. Kovner had "strayed far from the subject of this trial." Hausner should have controlled the witness and eliminated the portions of his testimony that were "not relevant." Landau warned him not to place the court "in such a situation" again. Hausner, visibly nonplussed, protested that his summation would demonstrate the testimony's relevance. Landau would have none of it. Hausner's indictment was the framework for the trial and he could not now add extraneous matters. Hausner, unwilling to concede, argued that the judges might not be fully aware of all he "intend[ed] to bring" to the court. An exasperated Landau cut off the exchange by noting, with decided condescension, "We heard your opening address which, it seems to me, lays down the general line of what you wish to place before the court." With that, Landau ended the session.[28]

Landau's attacks on Hausner's expansive view of what was relevant did not end with this exchange. For much of the remainder of the trial, Hausner was in the court's crosshairs. Such was the case when Zvi Zimmerman, a Knesset member and Ben-Gurion's political ally, testified. Given the nature of his testimony, there is good reason to assume that Hausner had been under political pressure to include him. He had little to add, and his testimony came late in the trial. If Hausner's objective was to give Zimmerman a platform, his efforts backfired. Zimmerman enraged Judge Landau by engaging in long discourses on his role in the underground even though the judge asked him not to do so. When he claimed to have heard about Eichmann from Gestapo men, Landau exploded. "The value of this evidence is, shall we say, next to nothing. . . . This is, in fact, gossip."[29]

After the resistance fighters' testimony, Hausner continued to paint a picture of the wider European tragedy. Most of the focus was on Eastern Europe, with virtually no mention of how the Holocaust spilled over into North Africa. There was little relief from the familiar story line: an overwhelmed Jewish population poised against an Eichmann-devised deportation system fully committed to ensnaring every Jew. Then into this unrelenting saga of grief and terror came a brief moment of emotional respite. Werner Melchior, son of Denmark's chief rabbi, described the rescue of Danish Jewry. He related how bishops, ambulance drivers, fishermen, housewives, neighbors, and strangers facilitated the escape of these seven thousand Jews—almost the entire Danish Jewish community—to Sweden. Shortly before being ferried across the strait, Melchior, demonstrating what some might consider an aggravated sense of responsibility, went to the university to return library books. At the entrance, students whom he knew in passing stopped him. "In case there is anything at all which you think we can reasonably do . . . you can get in touch with us." This, Melchior testified, happened not once but twice in the space of ten minutes. "During the preceding three and a half years of the occupation, there was not a single moment when the population was united so closely together" as during the rescue of the Jews. (After this rescue it was Eichmann who was dispatched to Denmark to determine precisely how this had happened and to prevent it from occurring again someplace else.) At last, into this Jerusalem courtroom, had come the uplift for which so many had thirsted. Haim Gouri described it as "artificial respiration." Jews in the courtroom were reminded that they had not been *completely* abandoned. One woman was weeping. Asked why she was crying now: "I cry whenever someone is kind to me."[30]

During this long succession of witnesses, Servatius, who was supposed to be defending Eichmann, was hamstrung. Well aware that he was unlikely to garner sympathy for his client by aggressively challenging those who had endured such harrowing experiences, he conducted almost no cross-examinations. When he did challenge a witness's testimony, his goal was to demonstrate that it bore no relevance to Eichmann's activities. Leon Wells told of Operation 1005, the group of Jewish prisoners assigned to eradicate the evidence by opening mass graves and exhuming, burning, and pulverizing the bodies. Servatius objected and argued that Wells could not connect Eichmann to this operation.

Furthermore, all the information Wells was imparting was already documented and well known. Though the judges rejected Servatius's complaint, they did put Hausner on notice that he had to demonstrate the "personal responsibility of the Accused for the act." Servatius had more latitude when cross-examining witnesses who were not survivors. During the testimony of an Israeli diplomat who had reviewed the eleven-thousand-page diary of Hans Frank, head of the Generalgouvernement, that area of Poland in which the death camps were located, Hausner had the witness expound on what Frank had called "our war against the Jews." Servatius asked but one question: "Was Adolf Eichmann's name mentioned in these twenty-nine volumes?" It was not. Servatius, having made his point, sat down. Servatius took the same approach with Judge Michael Musmanno. Immediately after the war, the United States Navy sent Musmanno to interview leading Nazis. He subsequently served as a judge at Nuremberg. According to Musmanno, the Nazi officials he interviewed all mentioned Eichmann's "powerful and authoritative hand" in the Final Solution. Servatius suggested that these Nazis were trying to shift the blame to Eichmann. Musmanno insisted that Eichmann's name had come up incidentally. Servatius, correctly dismissing this as hearsay, scored his point when he pointed out that at Nuremberg Musmanno presided over a murder trial for twenty-three defendants. Though a number of them testified about Eichmann's role, "you yourself did not mention Eichmann in your judgment by so much as one word." Judge Landau buttressed Servatius's challenge when he asked whether Eichmann's name appeared in the book Musmanno wrote regarding his experiences. It did not.[31]

Servatius's cross-examination of Dr. Heinrich Grüber, Protestant dean of Berlin, was less productive. During the war, Grüber, then a parson at a Berlin church, frequently intervened with Eichmann on Jews' behalf. Eventually he was imprisoned and tortured in Sachsenhausen and Dachau for his actions. He described Eichmann to the court as "a block of ice, or a block of marble, and everything you tried to get through to him just bounced off him." During the cross-examination, Servatius posited that Eichmann's animus toward the Jews was no different from the attitude of respectable and distinguished segments of German society, including academic and church leaders. To illustrate his point, Servatius read from the *Berliner Evangelisches Sonntagsblatt* (Berlin Evangelical Sunday Gazette). Showing its satisfaction with the regime's anti-Semitism, the paper observed that in all "the dark events of the past fifteen years the Jewish element played a leading role." Regarding the April 1933 government-sponsored boycott of Jewish stores, the paper celebrated the fact that now there would be "a containment of Jewish influence in Germany's public life. Nobody will seriously be able to object to this." Given that such sentiments, Servatius continued, were harbored by scholars and respected members of German society, shouldn't Eichmann, who never finished high school, have been justified in thinking they were correct? How could he be condemned for views that were espoused by leading members of society? Grüber would have none of it. It was one thing, he told Servatius, to be enthusiastic about National Socialism in 1933, and quite another to facilitate murder, as Eichmann had done.[32]

Grüber's testimony also gave expression to something quite chilling about contemporary Germany. It illustrated the extent to which the anti-Semitic views which were fundamental to National Socialism were still extant there. Grüber mentioned, but declined to name, a German who had helped Jews during the war. Grüber explained that the man was still alive, and he wanted to "spare him" any trouble. Judge Halevi, troubled by these comments, asked Grüber if it was not considered an "honor today that one risked oneself to rescue people?" The churchman explained that he was speaking from experience. When the German press reported that he was to testify against Eichmann, he had received a "thick file" of "threatening . . . [and] insulting letters" from fellow Germans. Before stepping down, the pastor, who had been so badly beaten in the concentration camp that when he returned he could not ascend the stairs without assistance, asked to make a personal statement. As "the first German [citizen] to stand before this high court and one who has found it hard to come here . . . my heartfelt entreaty [is] that we see to it that forgiving love [in Israel] and forgiven sin [in Germany] shall meet before the throne of God." Spectators wept. Israelis showered him with thank-you notes. One Foreign Ministry official observed that the Israeli public embraced Grüber as a sign that there was "no need to cry 'despair' over the human race and the Christian world." Martha Gellhorn, writing in *The Atlantic*

Monthly, put it more succinctly, though a bit hyperbolically: "One good man redeemed a nation."[33] He may not have redeemed a nation, particularly one in which people who saved Jews still had to hide their deeds, but he injected a note of hope into the hearts of many people.

It was in Hungary in 1944 that Adolf Eichmann reached the pinnacle or the abyss—depending on one's perspective— of his career. In the space of two months, with portions of Hungary on the verge of being liberated by the Soviets, Eichmann organized the dispatch of 437,000 Hungarian Jews to Auschwitz-Birkenau. Approximately 75 percent of them, about 330,000, were gassed. The fate of Eichmann's deportees gave Auschwitz its legendary status in the annals of genocide. The crematoria, despite having been designed to burn multiple bodies simultaneously, could not handle the load. Fire pits were used to supplement the ovens. The smoke from them was so intense that it was visible in the reconnaissance pictures taken by American planes.

Until 1944, Hungary, despite being Germany's ally, had balked at deporting Jews. As the Final Solution entered its final year, Hungarian Jews were still safe in their homes. Then, in March, Germany learned that Hungary, concerned about the Axis's deteriorating military situation, was contemplating switching sides. Hitler gave Admiral Horthy, head of the Hungarian government, an ultimatum: accept a German-approved government or be deposed as regent. Horthy chose the former. Within hours, SS units entered the country. Among them was the Eichmannkommando, whose job it was to decimate the last large, intact Jewish population under German control. Eichmann had brought with him men who, in the course of rendering much of Europe *Judenrein*, had perfected the process of deporting large numbers of Jews and confiscating their property with little resistance from the victims and fewer protests from their neighbors. Eichmann had another asset—the enthusiastic cooperation of Hungarian authorities, who, in Eichmann's words, offered up the Jews "like sour beer." His men "could not work fast enough."[34] But first Eichmann had to win the cooperation of Jewish leaders; and given his skills at deception and their propensity for being deceived, it turned out to be a relatively simple task. He summoned them to a meeting where, according to the stenographic notes taken by one of the participants, he gave what Hilberg has aptly described as "one of the greatest shows of his career." He began with directives. Within five days, all Hungarian Jews must wear yellow stars. No one was to travel without his personal approval. People evicted from their homes could live with relatives. The leaders were to create a Jewish Council to control the Jews' finances, oversee educational activities, establish a newspaper, and conduct a census. Then he reassured them. If the thousands of Jews already incarcerated in terrible conditions at the Kistarcsa concentration camp "behaved," improvements would be made. Jews who "volunteered" for labor in the Reich would receive "good treatment." If there were insufficient volunteers, the Jewish Council should draft them. But if the draftees "showed a proper attitude, no harm would befall them." Then he promised that anything Germans took from the Jews would eventually be returned or compensated for. After the war, "Jews would be free to do whatever they wanted . . . and . . . the Germans would again become good natured and permit everything as in the past." He closed with a warning. If Jews complied, "they would come to no harm . . . would be protected and enjoy the same treatment and pay as other workers." He would punish "most severely" anyone who molested them, including German soldiers. Given that he was already planning deportations to Auschwitz, the audacity of his lies was breathtaking. The leaders, either assuaged by Eichmann or believing they had no option, created a Judenrat (Jewish Council), which, after meeting with Eichmann's approval, directed the local communities to obey their instructions.[35]

The roundups were scheduled to begin on the first day of Passover. The Hungarians wanted to start in Budapest. Eichmann, demonstrating his expertise, suggested that they begin in the Carpathian east, where Hungary's more religious Hasidic Jews lived. This would prevent two of Eichmann's concerns from coming to fruition. Eichmann felt he could prevent a Warsaw Ghetto–like uprising by leading Budapest's more assimilated Jews into thinking that only insular Orthodox Jews were being targeted. It would also prevent a repetition of what had happened in Denmark, where the Jews, warned about the forthcoming deportations, had escaped to Sweden. If Jews in the east saw Budapest Jews being deported, they might flee toward the approaching Soviets. With Eichmann's men in the background, the Hungarians conducted a well-orchestrated reign of terror. Witnesses described for the court how the Jews were packed into temporary ghettos in brickyards, open fields, sausage factories, or stone quarries, where they waited, often with no roofs over their heads and minimal food or water. Hungarian Jew Martin Földi told the court that a Gestapo officer had declared, *"Ihr lebt ja hier wie die Schweine"*—"Here you live like pigs." They would live like that until the deportations to Auschwitz began in early May.[36]

Hausner then turned to a remarkable course of events. Not long after arriving in Hungary, German officials began ransom negotiations with Jewish leaders. Eichmann quickly took control of this effort and promised to exchange Jews in return for trucks and money. Though aspects of the "blood for goods" negotiations remain obscure, the Germans probably never intended to free any Jews. This may well have been Himmler's ploy to open negotiations with the British and Americans, make peace on the Western front, and leave the Soviets fighting on their own. Even if the Allies rejected such a deal, the Germans could leak word of it, thereby straining relations with the Soviets. The Germans could also blame the Allies for anything that happened to Hungarian Jewry by claiming that the Germans "offered them" to the Allies, who refused to accept them. That the entire effort was a sham is demonstrated by the fact that, while the negotiations "progressed," the Germans were murdering Jews at such a rate that, even if the Allies had agreed, there would have been virtually no one left to rescue. Joel Brand, one of the Jewish "negotiators," described to the court his first encounter with Eichmann.

> I approached the table. . . . Eichmann stood in front of it, legs astride, with his hands on his hips [and he] bellowed at me. You . . . do you know who I am? I am in charge of the *Aktion*. In Europe, Poland, Czechoslovakia, Austria it has been completed; now it is Hungary's turn.

He was prepared to "sell me a million Jews—goods for blood"—and threatened that if he did not receive a positive reply within three days he would "operate the mills at Auschwitz." In mid-May, Brand left Budapest for Istanbul and then Palestine, where he was to transmit the German ransom "offer" to Jewish leaders. On the same day, Eichmann also left Budapest. He, however, headed to Auschwitz, to ascertain that the camp was prepared for the Jews he was poised to dispatch for extermination. When Auschwitz Commandant Rudolph Höss complained that he could not "process" such large numbers into the camp, Eichmann suggested that they all be gassed.[37]

After a short stay in Istanbul, Brand reached Egypt, where the British arrested him as a spy. Jewish leaders hoped they would at least give the appearance of contemplating the offer, which might slow the deportation process. The British refused. In the interim, Eichmann continued his so-called negotiations with Israel Kasztner and Brand's wife, Hansi. Though many people, including Judge Halevi, would condemn Kasztner for negotiating with Eichmann and selling out Hungarian Jews, this had been anything but a level playing field. To speak of it as "collaboration" is to misrepresent what it really was: a desperate attempt to stall and possibly prevent mass murder. At one meeting, Kasztner rose to leave before having been officially dismissed. Eichmann exploded at what he considered to be a tremendous impertinence. "Kasztner, I shall send you off to convalesce at Theresienstadt or perhaps you would prefer Auschwitz?" Eichmann continued: "Hear me, I must clean out the provincial towns from this Jewish dirt [shit], no arguments and no crying will help here."

Hansi Brand testified that she had met Eichmann over a dozen times. She soon learned that whenever he promised something "there was always a convenient excuse" for him not to keep his word. "He kept stressing that what a German officer promises, he will always honor. But he did not honor anything." Many Hungarian Jews remained convinced that the Judenrat members and Kasztner in particular—who, though he was not a member of the Judenrat, directly negotiated with Eichmann—had failed them miserably during this period. They accused Kasztner and the others of knowing the Jews' fate but failing to warn them. When Hungarian Judenrat member Pinchas Freudiger testified, this anger erupted in open court. A spectator began shouting and accusing Freudiger of being responsible for the death of his family. Landau demanded silence, and the spectator was hustled from the courtroom. But the "damage" was done. With this outburst, shades of the Kasztner trial and its accusations against the Jewish Councils had found their way into the courtroom. The public gallery was not the sole source of such "intrusions." They also came from the bench. Judge Halevi, whose very presence was a stark reminder of that trial, asked Hansi Brand whether her committee had considered assassinating Eichmann. Implicit in his question was the accusation that those at the top, the leaders who knew precisely what faced their fellow Jews, had failed to take actions that might have stopped the process. Brand seemed flummoxed by Halevi's question. She recognized, as he seemed not to, that such action would probably not have materially changed matters. "Let us assume . . . one of us shoots him. What would we achieve by that? . . . We were a Committee for the Aid and Rescue of our people. . . . We were not heroes. So what we bore in mind was how we could try to keep people alive."[38]

When Margit Reich took the stand, she brought something with her that bore vivid witness to Hungarian Jews' desperate state. Her husband had written her a letter that he threw from the train on which he was being deported to Auschwitz. He had scrawled on the outside, "Blessed be the hand which posts this letter." Some hand did post it, and Margit received it. Precisely seventeen years later, it was read in Jerusalem: "My dear wife and children . . . We are setting out upon a very long journey. . . . I shall somehow bear my fate whatever it may be. I do not want to make you sad but I would want very much to live yet in your midst. May God grant us that we may be allowed to achieve that." He never returned. Reich, emotionally unable to read the letter herself, had asked Assistant Prosecutor Gabriel Bach to read it for her. He was so overwhelmed that he found it hard to continue.

Martin Földi described for the court how at Birkenau he had one last glimpse of his wife and children, who had been sent to the "left"—that is, the gas chambers. He recalled that, despite the crush of people, he could identify them because of his little girl's red coat. "The red spot was a sign that my wife was near there. The red spot was getting smaller and smaller. . . ." He never saw them again.[39] Years later, that coat would reappear in Steven Spielberg's film *Schindler's List*.

As news of the deportations spread, the Red Cross and foreign governments decried them. Uncharacteristically, even the Pope spoke out against them, though he did so without mentioning the Jews. In early July, approximately eight weeks after the deportations had begun, Horthy, afraid of his fate in the hands of the Allies, ordered them stopped. Furious, Eichmann sent his men to Kistarcsa to ship a thousand Jews to Auschwitz. The Judenrat alerted sympathetic Hungarian authorities, who stopped the train. Undeterred, Eichmann struck again a few days later. This time, however, he engaged in a bit of subterfuge. He summoned the Judenrat to his headquarters and kept them incommunicado for the day. In the interim, his men returned to Kistarcsa and deported fifteen hundred Jews. When the train crossed the border into Poland, Eichmann released the leaders from his headquarters. A few days later, he shipped yet another trainload of Jews to Auschwitz.

Hausner was anxious to prove to the court that, in addition to facilitating murder from behind his desk, Eichmann had actually committed murder with his own hands. He contended that, while in Hungary, Eichmann had shot a little boy who had been trying to steal some fruit from the orchard outside his villa. Given the abundance of documents that implicated Eichmann, it is interesting that Hausner felt compelled to prove that Eichmann had personally killed someone. Hausner had not included this specific act in the indictment because, he explained to the court, he saw no need to set the boy "apart from all the millions." His objective in raising it was to demonstrate to the court the nature of Eichmann's character. But, the historian Stephan Landsman has rightfully asked, can or should one be convicted for having a vile and nefarious character? Ultimately, Hausner's efforts regarding the murder were thwarted when questions posed by both Servatius and the judges proved that Avraham Gordon, whom Hausner called as the witness to the murder, could not have observed it.[40]

Facing international protests for their collaboration with the Nazis in the annihilation of the Jews, the Hungarian government agreed to release forty thousand Jews to the Swiss, who would allow them to immigrate to Palestine. Furious, Eichmann instructed a subordinate, "Everything possible should be done, in order to delay . . . and prevent" such "biologically valuable material" from entering Palestine. Upon learning that Hitler supported this plan, Eichmann demonstrated what Cesarani has aptly described as an "astonishing degree of presumption for a Lieutenant-

Colonel" and decided to ask him to reconsider. The prosecution introduced a letter by German ambassador Veesenmayer, who Eichmann claimed wielded ultimate power in Hungary, describing how Eichmann proposed sabotaging these efforts by deporting "suddenly and speedily" those who might qualify for emigration. Veesenmayer's communiqué depicts Eichmann as someone who was far more than just a transportation specialist. "It has been agreed with Eichmann that [if] . . . additional evacuations of Jews from Budapest will be approved, they are to be started as suddenly as possible and carried out with such speed that the Jews in question will already have been deported before the formalities have been completed."[41] When some Jews managed to obtain immigration permits to Spain, Eichmann contemplated waylaying them as they passed through France. During the final throes of the Final Solution, he remained more committed to its execution than were his superiors. Horthy, under pressure from extremist elements in his government, agreed to restart the deportations on August 25. On the 19th, Eichmann, possibly afraid that the Hungarians might renege, pressed for them to begin sooner. Then the pro-German government in Romania fell. The Romanians left the Axis and joined the Allied side. Horthy, assuming that the Axis were going to lose the war, canceled the deportations.

Throughout this period, Eichmann kept pushing for faster extermination of the Jews. Himmler saw matters differently and put the decision about restarting the deportations on hold. This did not represent an ideological change regarding the murder of the Jews: the Final Solution could be restarted once the military situation was stabilized. Himmler was also apparently persuaded by his own regime's propaganda regarding the power of the Jews. He speculated that American and British Jews could convince the Western Allies to make a separate peace with Germany. Eichmann, recognizing that his task was thwarted at this point, returned to Berlin. Then, in mid-October, the Germans engineered a coup by the pro-Nazi Hungarian organization, the Arrow Cross. Within two days, Eichmann returned to Budapest. He summoned Kasztner. The Soviets were already on Hungarian soil, and the Reich was crumbling. Nonetheless, Eichmann greeted Kasztner with noticeable bluster.

> So you see I am back here again! You no doubt thought that the story of Romania and Bulgaria would repeat itself here? Apparently you forgot that Hungary still rests in the shadow of the destruction of the Reich! And our hands are long enough to grasp the Jews of Budapest as well. . . .

He then proposed a deal. Budapest Jews would be deported to the Reich, "this time on foot." But if the Jews "place at our disposal a suitable number of trucks," they would go by truck. Behind Eichmann's "offer" lay Berlin's desperate need for laborers. The Hungarians agreed to transfer fifty thousand Jews to Germany to "replace worn-out Russian and other POW's." In the past, when "offered" a portion of a country's Jews, Eichmann had refused: for him it was all or nothing. This time, he accepted. In truth, he had not retreated from his all-encompassing approach. Accord-ing to a German Foreign Office report, he intended to keep asking for groups of fifty thousand until he had "secure[d] the final objective of clearing the Hungarian zone."[42]

He began with a vengeance. The court heard how he had rounded up and dispatched tens of thousands of Jews on week-long marches, often with no food, blankets, or water. Conditions were so barbaric that some of the marchers committed suicide. Swiss diplomats, who witnessed the marches, reported that those who became sick "were often shot dead . . . [or] were left behind . . . without medical help; only in rare cases were arrangements made for feeding them." The marchers "received at most 3 to 4 portions of soup throughout the entire duration of the foot march, but usually went several days without receiving any food at all." The horror of the conditions is best attested to by the reac-tion of Waffen-SS General Hans Jüttner and Auschwitz Commandant Höss when they passed the marchers on the road. "Shocked" by the "terrifying impression" made by the marchers, they "protested sharply" and ordered the marches halted, because they feared the inmates would be unable to work upon reaching Germany. When Eichmann returned to Budapest, he ordered the marches resumed, arguing that they had been halted on the "mistaken impression of some gentlemen who were not capable of judging whether people who had been on the road for about seven or eight days could be regarded as fit for labor." During his interrogation with Captain Less, Eichmann painted a markedly different pic-ture of the marchers: "Not many died, apart from . . . a few

[who] died naturally." Speaking as if he had no direct connection with the marches, he lamented them as a "sad business" and asked Less if he did not think "it was sad when citizens walk in this manner, stagger along in this fashion, is that not so, for the final kilometers?" He also insisted that he "never looked at these wretched scenes on principle, unless I received an order." He did not elucidate the precise nature of that principle.[43]

With the Russians approaching, Eichmann had his men ferret out Jews who were being protected by foreign delegations. He told Red Cross workers that, if he could, he would shoot "the Jewish dog Wallenberg" for sheltering Jews. But he was not able to accomplish this goal, or that of ridding Hungary of all its Jews; and in November, after the Hungarians stopped the foot marches, Eichmann, aware that the end was near, left for Berlin. The Germans were gone, but for Jews the horrors continued. The Hungarian Arrow Cross, the National Socialist group that had assumed control of the government in October, barbarically murdered thousands of Jews who had survived the Nazis. Some were tied together and pushed into the Danube. This orgy of torture and murder lasted until the Soviets arrived in February 1945. Lozowick has aptly described it as "a malevolent blood fest." Eichmann had gone to Hungary intent on organizing "a deportation, surpassing every preceding operation in magnitude." He succeeded. Over a half-million Hungarian Jews had died from poor conditions or had been murdered. In the space of less than eight weeks, approximately 145 trains had left for Auschwitz carrying about 440,000 Jews. Tens of thousands of others died during the marches to the Reich or from barbaric treatment while still in Hungary. Even though during the trial Hausner attributed to Eichmann parts of the Final Solution for which he bore no responsibility, when it came to describing the murder of Hungarian Jewry the prosecution got it just about right.[44]

After addressing the tragedy of Hungarian Jewry, Hausner attempted to link the Holocaust to contemporary Middle Eastern politics. He argued that Eichmann and the Grand Mufti of Jerusalem, Hajj Amin al Husseini, were closely connected. The mufti, who had been a guest of the Reich in Berlin during the war, helped organize a Muslim unit of the SS, tried to galvanize other Muslims to fight the Allies, and insisted that the Reich take the harshest actions possible against Jews. In 1943, after learning of the murder of European Jewry, the mufti declared that Germany had "decided to find a final solution to the Jewish danger that would remove their harm from the world." There is no question about his approval for the Nazi effort to murder Jews. His close relationship with Eichmann, however, was not clear from the evidence. Eichmann had boasted to Kasztner that he was "a personal friend of the Grand Mufti." An entry from the mufti's diary appears to praise Eichmann as a "rare diamond." Eichmann admitted that he had met the mufti. Though the mufti probably deeply appreciated the work in which Eichmann's office was engaged, there was probably only a slight personal connection between them.

There certainly was no evidence to support Hausner's implication that they had a close relationship and had worked together.[45] What was clear, without Hausner's explicitly saying so, was that this was an expression of Ben-Gurion's conviction that the Arab nations were the heirs to the Nazi desire to destroy as many Jews as possible.

Hausner concluded his case with a last-ditch effort to introduce the transcripts of the Sassen tapes. Because the tapes themselves were unavailable and the transcripts could not be matched against them, the court ruled that they did "not have any value as a document." It did admit into evidence the pages Eichmann had corrected or on which he had added additional comments in his own handwriting. Hausner read a selection of those additions. Eichmann had told Sassen that it "was Hitler himself—neither Heydrich nor Himmler" who initiated the Wannsee Conference. At this gathering the state secretaries of those departments responsible for policies relating to Jews were informed by Heydrich of the details of the Final Solution. They discussed the way in which this murder program would proceed and concluded that it would target approximately eleven million European Jews, including those from England, Ireland, and Spain. After the meeting Eichmann sat with Müller and Heydrich, "not in order to talk shop, but in order to relax after the long hours of strain." These comments made it plain that Hitler and Nazi Germany stood behind the Final Solution, but Eichmann's most self-incriminating words came when he recalled his "work" in Hungary. Nazis who tried to stop the mass murders had "sinned against German blood." He, on the other hand, had reached "deportation figures to be proud of," something he credited to his "uncompromising fanaticism." Yet he lamented that he did "not achieve my ultimate aim, which was to free Hungary of all its Jews."[46] It was not an auspicious moment for Eichmann. He had been damned with his own words.

5

O n June 20, ten weeks after the Jerusalem courtroom was first called to order, Adolf Eichmann "took the stand"—actually, he stayed in his booth—in his own defense. The disembodied voice of the rambling, self-incriminating witness of the Bureau 06 interrogation, and the boastful, unapologetic, slightly inebriated memoirist of the Sassen tapes, were replaced by a disciplined and well-prepared defendant.

During an eight-day recess, he and Servatius had carefully mapped their strategy. Rather than ignore the incriminating evidence Hausner had introduced, they would attack it head-on and attempt to explain it away. Their explanations fell into certain predictable categories. Eichmann was obliged to follow orders. He never acted on his own initiative: "I made absolutely sure to get instructions from my chief on even the most minor matters." Some of the documents that incriminated him had been altered by other Nazis in an attempt to shift the blame to him. Other documents were simply wrong and resulted from sloppy work by his colleagues. Sometimes one explanation was piled on top of another. Such was the case when Eichmann addressed the memo by the Foreign Office's Franz Rademacher regarding Belgrade Jews. In it Rademacher noted in the margin: "Eichmann suggests shooting." Eichmann insisted that Rade-macher was wrong. Such a recommendation "would have gone far beyond my area of competence." Moreover, Eich-mann insisted, Rademacher was incompetent and had incor-rectly entered his name. On those occasions during his testimony when none of these excuses sufficed, Eichmann fell back on faulty memory. He did not remember the telegram he had sent to the Security Police in France order-ing that "the Jew Golub," who had just received a valid pass-port for a South American country, thereby making him eligible to emigrate, be immediately arrested and placed on an "evacuation transport" to Auschwitz, to keep him from leaving. Nor did he remember the request from Strasbourg University's "Institute of Ancestral Heredity" for 115 skele-tons for research. Eichmann had arranged for these Jews to be selected by an anthropologist and gassed. He could not deny his involvement, since the letter explicitly referred to his discussions about it. Meshing two excuses, he insisted that he had forgotten, but even if he had participated, he would not have made the decision, because he was not "com-petent or authorized to deal with these matters."[1] Actually, Eichmann may have been telling the truth in both of these cases. He was consulted on Serbia, but did not in fact have any authority there. By the same token, while he may have lobbied on behalf of Strasbourg University, the request and decision would have gone through a different chain of com-mand and been made at a higher level than Eichmann.

Eichmann had yet one other explanation, which court-room spectators invariably greeted with derisive laughter:

He was no anti-Semite. He had "worked *with* Jews" to extricate them from the problems they faced. His work in Vienna did not oppress Austrian Jews but was "beneficial" to them, because, he explained using Nazi-like terminology, "two thirds of the Jews domiciled in Austria could be brought to emigrate." He conveniently ignored the reason Austrian Jews wished to leave, which was what he and his colleagues were doing to them. His decision that Jews who were to be "evacuated"—his euphemism for "deported"—had to place almost all their resources in a special fund was in the "interests of both parties," Germans and Jews. These "donations" sustained those who remained behind. He was an ally of the Jews and, as such, "facilitate[d] and promote[d]" Zionism by striving to "put the Jews on their feet in their own land." Breaking with his repeated claim that he had never taken any initiative on his own, he claimed—falsely—that he had conceived of the idea for a Madagascar settlement. He drew his inspiration, he told the court, from Herzl's Zionist classic, *The Jewish State.* His "sole" objective was that "land be placed under the feet of the Jews." He did more, he told the court, than try to resettle the Jews in a homeland. He saved their lives. In September 1941, he deported twenty thousand Jews to the Łódź Ghetto instead of to the "East," despite the intense objections of the German officials there. He did so because he had seen the "preparations for extermination" in the East, knew the fate awaiting them there, and wanted to save them.[2]

Servatius then turned to Eichmann's role at the January 1942 Wannsee Conference, which Heydrich had convened to brief other ministries on the Final Solution. Eichmann had previously claimed that he wrote Heydrich's speech, and that after the meeting Heydrich and Gestapo Chief Müller had accorded him the honor of inviting him to join them for a fireside celebratory Cognac. Now he spun things differently, claiming that, as secretary, he had simply prepared the statistical information for the meeting and compiled the minutes afterward. Regarding the fireside Cognac, he "was allowed to be present" while they celebrated. If he had played such a minor role, Servatius asked, why had he told Sassen how pleased he was with the conference? He was pleased, he explained, because he recognized that the awful "solution" that had been discussed at the meeting was not his plan, in that he was not "personally connected" with it. In contrast to the murder program, he had always sought "peaceful solutions," which did "not require such a violent and drastic solution of bloodshed." He turned to the bench and added a bizarre addendum. Roman procurator Pontius Pilate, despite having convicted Jesus, believed himself to be "entirely innocent of any guilt" because he had been ordered to do something and did it. So, too, Eichmann declared, his superiors, whom Eichmann called the "Popes," had ordered him, and it "was up to me to obey." It is entirely fanciful to imagine that he contemplated issues of guilt and innocence in 1942. Moreover, he seemed oblivious that he was making this historical comparison but a stone's throw from where Pilate's sentencing of Jesus had been carried out, and that he was doing so before a court composed of Jews, whom the New Testament held accountable for Jesus' fate.

The dense nature of his observation was compounded by the fact that church leaders had consistently used this event to generate the very Jew hatred that was at the heart of what was being adjudicated at this trial. Without the legacy of contempt nurtured by the church, the Final Solution would never have been realized. Was Eichmann completely deaf and blind to the identity of those before whom he was testifying or was this an attempt—conscious or unconscious— by him, who grew up with daily Bible readings, to cast the Jews as once again being the crucifiers? Irrespective of Eichmann's motivations, with this comment the historical narrative of the trial seemed to come full circle.[3]

This was not the only time Eichmann seemed oblivious to how strange his explanations sounded. Servatius asked him about a directive he had issued ordering that trains deporting Jews carry a minimum of one thousand people, even though their capacity was for only seven hundred. Eichmann claimed that the seven-hundred figure was calculated on the basis of soldiers with baggage. Since Jews' luggage was sent separately, there was room for an additional three hundred people. The gallery erupted in laughter. Servatius also asked him about his superiors' refusal to allow him to hire a rabbi to teach him Hebrew. They rejected his request, Eichmann claimed, because they feared a rabbi might influence him. They were also reluctant to pay the paltry hourly fee of three marks. Eichmann may have thought this incident would establish for the court that, had he been as important as the prosecution asserted, his superiors would have neither feared the rabbi's influence nor objected to such a meager expenditure. Had he stopped there, the anecdote would have done him no harm. But, inexplicably, he continued, and wistfully observed, "It would have been best had I proposed that a rabbi be arrested so that he could give me instruction from the prison. But I had not thought of this." One can imagine how the German Jews present, some of whom might have been candidates for arrest, reacted to his lament. He had shown similar obtuseness during his interrogation by Police Inspector Less. Eichmann had inquired about the fate of Less's family. When Less told him that his father had been on the last deportation from Berlin and had eventually been murdered in Auschwitz, Eichmann responded in a manner suggesting that this was something with which he was unconnected: "But that's horrible, Herr Hauptmann! That's horrible!"[4]

When he turned to Hungary, Servatius faced a special challenge. Elsewhere in Europe, Eichmann had operated from afar and was generally not present during deportations. In Hungary, not only was he there but, lest there be any doubt about his role, he headed an SS unit dubbed "Sonderkommando Eichmann." Eichmann's version of events there differed dramatically from Hausner's. Rather than playing a pivotal role, he claimed he was only "marginally involved," did not conduct confiscations, make arrests, or even establish deportation timetables. After Eichmann delineated all he did *not* do, Servatius asked the obvious: "What was left for you?" Acknowledging that it sounded "incredible," Eichmann insisted he was "simply an observer" assigned to keep his Berlin bosses informed about

Hungarian matters. Why, then, Servatius asked, did German ambassador Veesenmayer write Foreign Minister Ribbentrop that "Head of Special Jewish Operations Unit Security Service, SS Obersturmbannführer Eichmann," opposed letting some Jews immigrate to Palestine even though he had been told that Hitler favored this. If Eichmann's role was so inconsequential, why did his opinion matter? Eichmann insisted he was simply relaying Himmler's orders. If he played such a menial role, why, Servatius asked, did Dr. Theodor Horst Grell, the head of the Foreign Office's Jewish Affairs Section in Hungary, describe him as "exclusively responsible for the technical implementation of transport of Jews"? Why did Grell say that Eichmann had told him sometime in late 1944 that "he had some six million people on his conscience"? Eichmann insisted he could not have said this, because he did not have "anyone's death on his conscience."[5]

How, Servatius asked, could he explain his role in the "blood for goods" negotiations? A savvy defendant, Eichmann knew that, after repeatedly insisting that he had only followed orders, he could not now contend that in 1944 he had initiated a massive plan to save Jews. Instead, he claimed it was his attempt to even the score with an SS rival, who had encroached on his territory by trying to exchange Jews for military goods. "Furious," he decided to conduct the negotiations himself and to expand the offer to a million Jews. He denied having told Brand that if he did not receive a positive reply to his ransom offer he would restart the gas chambers, because controlling the killings was not within his "competence." Ironically, at least a portion of his testimony was probably true. He could not start or halt the killings at will. However, he might have told Brand precisely what was reported. It would not have been the first time that he inflated claims about his powers. In France in 1942, when an official canceled a few deportations, an irate Eichmann threatened that if this happened again, he would halt the deportation of French Jews. This decision, too, was beyond his authority. He probably made the threat in order to ensure that the official would henceforth comply with his orders. In short, when it served his purposes, he painted himself as all-powerful. Now that he was on trial for his life, he offered a very different image. When he yelled and ranted at Brand, it was not because he wish to exert his power. He yelled because he was "hurt" and filled with "anger" that others were sabotaging his attempts to organize the emigration of Jews.[6]

As the examination drew to a close, Eichmann tried to impress upon the court his honesty and willingness to confront the truth. He knew that "some of the people" whom he deported would be "killed in the camps." Yet he had no choice: "I had to carry out the transports in accordance with my orders." Stressing his sincerity, he added, "That I must admit according to the truth." Eichmann concluded by lamenting his fate. He was "unlucky." Generals could "evad[e] service," whereas a person such as himself who held "an inferior position cannot shirk his duty." If he was guilty of anything, it was in the "ethical," not the legal context. His guilt was, he told the judges, a personal matter, which he had to address with his "innermost self." Obliterating the

Jews whose deaths he facilitated, he declared himself to be the victim, "a tool in the hands of stronger powers and stronger forces, and of an inexorable fate."

Time believed Eichmann had been "a good witness." *The Observer*, though convinced that "he would do it all again," believed he proved himself a "cleverer man" than the Israelis had assumed. Haim Gouri reacted to Eichmann's testimony with astonishment: "Not anger. Not pain. Not hatred. Just amazement." In his testimony, Eichmann had gone from a "logistics officer . . . to sergeant . . . to clerk, a mere secretary who passed on letters and telegrams from his superiors to his subordinates and from his subordinates to his superiors, up, down and sideways."[7] Gouri was unconvinced by this transformation. Others, foremost among them Hannah Arendt, saw things quite differently. She saw an automaton who was just passing on information and who failed to understand that what he had done was wrong.

Eichmann's loquaciousness infuriated the judges. Landau had to admonish him repeatedly to keep his answers short. "It is clear to us that, in German, the predicate comes at the end of the sentence, but it takes too long to reach the predicate." Matters did not improve. The judges complained about his tendency to give incomprehensible answers, deliver "speeches" rather than answers, and include irrelevant material. Even from a distance of nearly fifty years, Eichmann's testimony remains maddening. In response to Servatius's question about his insistence that foreign Jews wear the yellow star, Eichmann began a discourse on police regulations for official correspondence and interministerial rivalries. Exasperated, Landau interrupted and instructed him, "You were not asked to give a general lecture. . . . You were asked a specific question." Ignoring Landau's reprimand, Eichmann continued with a discourse on the procedure for drafting letters for the department chief's signature, including what the different-colored inks signified. Using German to ensure that Eichmann understood, an exasperated Landau lectured him: "You are asked specific questions and you must give specific answers. . . . Do you understand?"[8] Eichmann may have assumed that, by larding his answers with bureaucratic detail, he would project the image of an operations officer accused of acts well beyond his ken. If this was his plan, he enjoyed some success. *The New York Times* was struck that Eichmann did not appear "sullen or defiant," just "dull." Their coverage described him as a man who "reveled in bureaucratic phrases" and was not even "worth hating."[9] Yet some observers saw another side. As the examination proceeded, Servatius often stumbled, mixed up documents, and could not locate the proper reference. On occasion, Eichmann corrected him or passed him a document from his booth so he could make a particular point. When this happened, one observer noted, "Eichmann's voice sharpened: the cold snarl, the bark that many of the witnesses remembered was there, one tone beneath what we heard." The prominent French journalist Joseph Kessel described Eichmann's reaction when the prosecution read from depositions by his former SS colleagues that implicated him. Kessel felt the "passion and rage" emerging from beneath the "hollow mask." This, he declared, was the "true Eichmann."[10]

After Servatius concluded his examination came the long-awaited confrontation—"the battle of wits"—which the spectators who packed the courtroom had been anticipating: Hausner's cross-examination. The exchange—described by one observer as a "duel"—turned ugly from the outset. Hausner wanted yes or no replies to his questions. Instead, he got labyrinthine, expansive nonresponses. The attorney general's attempts to cut Eichmann off were to no avail. As the answers grew maddeningly more evasive, Hausner became increasingly frustrated. "The Accused was asked a question and he must answer it. . . . But he must not give replies in the form of lectures." When that did not help, Hausner began to hector and shout. At one point, just as Eichmann uttered the word "because," which was usually a precursor to one of his convoluted discourses, Hausner emphatically cut him off: "I don't want to hear any 'because.' I want an answer." Eichmann, seemingly oblivious to the attorney general's demand, plowed on. An exasperated Hausner exploded: "Without 'but,' I want an answer!" Landau immediately admonished Hausner that Eichmann must be allowed to finish. Though Hausner's combative style seemed beneath the dignity of both his office and this case, his frustrations were understandable. His plan was to build an evidentiary web around Eichmann and to box him in with one of two choices: either acknowledge what the evidence indicates you did, or deny it. If Eichmann did the former, he would be admitting his guilt. If he did the latter, particularly in light of evidence that so clearly implicated him, he would be exposing himself to the judges as a liar rather than the "honest defendant" he insisted he was.[11]

If Hausner was annoyed by Eichmann's evasive style and meandering nonanswers, he was incensed by Eichmann's assertion that he sought to help, not persecute, Jews. What documents, Hausner sneered, proved that "Jewish functionaries asked you to send Jews naked and penniless to Nisko?" Eichmann painted an idyllic portrait, one that was in stark contrast to the testimony offered by Nisko survivors. First Eichmann claimed that the Nisko plan had a benevolent motivation. He wanted to enable Jews to live "among themselves and not under the conditions of stress to which they were subjected in their previous localities." He spoke as if the "stress" was an inherent condition in which he had no role. He had done the same thing when he expressed his "horror" that Captain Less's father had been deported from Berlin and murdered in Auschwitz. His description of Nisko bore little relationship to reality: "Rivers, villages, markets, small towns . . . It would benefit all concerned." Hausner challenged Eichmann's bucolic description by observing that "even Polish farmers were unable to cultivate" land there, and no one drank the water because of fear of toxins. Eichmann, defending it as "not the worst," contended that it was "not that certain" that the waters were poisoned. At the most they "might cause

typhoid." Eichmann described himself as being "enthusiastic" about finding an area to "be allocated for these Jewish
needs." Had Hausner stopped at this point, the absurdity of
Eichmann's claim would have stood on its own. Instead, he
pushed further. "All you have related here . . . is a pack of
lies. . . . You knew that the Jews in the Generalgouvern[e]-
ment were facing extermination."[12] Now it was Hausner
who had gone too far. He was wrong: At the time of the
Nisko plan, Jews were not facing systematic extermination.
Many of those brought to Nisko died from the harsh conditions. If more would have been sent, they, too, would have
died. But this was not yet the Final Solution, the deliberate
destruction of European Jewry. Hausner made the same mistake when he insisted that 1939 meetings regarding the Final
Solution constituted planning sessions for genocide. At
that point, the Final Solution did not yet mean purposeful
murder.

Sometimes Eichmann scored small but direct hits. Hausner contended that, according to the Nuremberg documents, Julius Streicher had devised the Madagascar plan.
Eichmann countered that Hausner had it wrong: the
Nuremberg documents indicated that the Madagascar idea
had been mentioned in Streicher's paper, *Der Stürmer*, but
not that he had devised it. A small matter, but Hausner
could not have been happy to be corrected by Eichmann on a
document's factual content. A few seconds later, Hausner
suffered a more significant blow. When Eichmann claimed
that reading Herzl's *The Jewish State* inspired him to pro-
pose creating a Jewish territory, an overwrought Hausner

exploded: "You do not mention names of persons whom you are not fit or worthy of mentioning." Landau admonished Hausner for his inappropriate remark. Then Hausner continued to sink deeper into a morass of his own making. For some inexplicable reason, he again insisted that Eichmann had gotten the idea for Madagascar from *Der Stürmer.* Eichmann protested: "I was not a reader of the *Stürmer.*" Hausner, his voice laced with cynicism, responded: "You did not read the *Stürmer*? Your Führer used to read it every week." This kind of comment prompted the *Washington Post* to note, "The more Eichmann was needled by Hausner, the more dignity Eichmann displayed." Eichmann was hardly on trial for reading this anti-Semitic newspaper. And here, too, Eichmann may have been truthful. Eichmann's SD superiors considered Streicher's propaganda undignified, vulgar, and unproductive.[13]

Hausner soon suffered another public blow. As he was jousting with Eichmann, Servatius rose to object. Hausner turned to him and rather derisively said, "I would ask the Counsel for the Defense not to interfere in the course of the cross-examination." Landau immediately interceded: "Mr. Attorney General, you do not know yet what Counsel for the Defense wants to say." Then, sounding as if he were explaining courtroom procedure to a novice, he added, "This occurs in trials every day." Even though the judges rejected Servatius's objection, it was not a good moment for Hausner: he had won on content but lost on stature. It is hard to explain his outburst, given that even novice courtroom-watchers knew that such interruptions occur in a trial. Hausner may have unconsciously considered himself as more aligned *with* the judges than appearing *before* them. In fact, giving the lie to any notion that this was a "show trial," throughout the proceedings the judges clashed with Hausner. They had a far more traditional perception of the structure and limitations of the trial. Hausner wanted to tell the entire story of the Final Solution. They wanted a narrowly constructed judicial proceeding that focused on Eichmann's misdeeds, whereas Hausner wanted a broad educational exercise. They thought they were in charge; sometimes Hausner acted as if he was. This was not a result of Hausner's limited courtroom experience. It was a reflection of two conflicting perspectives on the goal of the proceedings. The judges' primary objective was to conduct a scrupulously fair legal proceeding that would win the respect of the world. Hausner's goal was to tell the story of the Holocaust in all its detail and, in so doing, to capture the imagination not just of Israel's youth and world Jewry, but of the entire world. Landau's frequent admonitions of Hausner and Eichmann's refusal to capitulate illustrate just how much of this case was out of the Israeli government's—read Ben-Gurion's—control.[14]

Hausner soon regained his footing. Eichmann had insisted that the notation *"im Auftrage"* ("by order of"), which appeared on each of his letters, demonstrated that "I had received the order . . . [and] was acting . . . on behalf of someone else." Hausner pointed out that Gestapo protocol stipulated that all correspondence include "i.A."—a required formula, it signified nothing. Then, yet again,

Hausner pushed too far. He introduced a letter Heydrich had written shortly after Wannsee. "Since happily now the basic design has been established with regard to the practical implementation of the Final Solution of the Jewish Question . . . I would ask you to instruct your official in charge to contact my Specialist Officer responsible for this matter, SS Obersturmbannführer Eichmann." Did this not demonstrate, Hausner asked, that Heydrich gave Eichmann a "free hand . . . to run Jewish affairs as he saw fit . . . ?" Once again Hausner overplayed his hand. Eichmann was Heydrich's "Specialist Officer" and, as such, handled many aspects of the Final Solution, but certainly not all of them, and, contrary to Hausner's contentions, he did not run Jewish affairs as he saw fit.[15] The documents in Hausner's hands proved that and nothing more.

Hausner was at his strongest when he maintained a steady pace and did not let himself be drawn into extended exchanges. A report submitted to Ribbentrop regarding the fate of Italian and Greek Jews began with the words "In the opinion of the Reich SS Leader—SS Obersturmbannführer Eichmann." Hausner asked Eichmann to explain this. After claiming that the Foreign Office wanted him to provide "a concrete expression" of Himmler's wishes, Eichmann tried to segue into a discourse on the transmission of information. Hausner stopped him. "Look at the document—this does not refer to any concrete expression of wishes." Rather lamely, Eichmann tried to shift the discussion to the deportation of Greek Jewry and argued that he had had no hand in that. Hausner stayed on point. "In an official document, which dates from the time of the War, at a time when no one could have intended to shift any blame on you, an official body describes you in a document submitted to Ribbentrop as the Reich SS Leadership [sic] in Jewish Affairs. How can you contest it?" Abandoning his claim that the Foreign Office wanted a "concrete expression" of Himmler's views, Eichmann contended that he did not need to contest the report because it was a "mistake and erroneous." A somewhat skeptical Judge Landau asked for clarification. If the attorney general was wrong, "then how and why does your name appear in the document?" Now Eichmann, rather lamely, claimed that this was a matter of "bureaucratic sloppiness." He had "passed on the information"; hence his name was mentioned. Hausner, having made his point, could have stopped here. Instead, he began to taunt Eichmann. Did he expect people to believe he was just "a messenger boy, a megaphone when the Foreign Ministry called you Reichsführung-SS?" It was Judge Halevi who, without taunts or sarcasm, cut to the heart of the matter. He called Eichmann's attention to one word. The document did not say, "According to information from the Reich SS Leadership; it says 'In the *opinion* of'. How do you explain this?" In what seemed like a reflexive action, Eichmann blamed Rademacher, the Ministry of Justice official who had dictated the document: he was a "very slipshod bureaucrat."[16]

Some court watchers kept waiting for Hausner to elicit from Eichmann an unambiguous admission of guilt and contended that because he never did, he failed. They thought that Hausner should "give up" because Eichmann was best-ing him.[17] In fact, these exchanges revealed Eichmann to be both a wily and a desperate man, ready to pile excuse on top of excuse. As I read them, I was reminded of David Irving's behavior at my own trial. When my barrister presented him with a document that conclusively demonstrated that he had misrepresented the truth—that is, lied—he would initially try to reinterpret it. When that failed, as it invariably did, he would cite other documents to try to prove his point. When they, too, contradicted his version of events, he would try yet some other avenue of escape. When all had failed and he was completely boxed in by the evidence, he would turn to the judge and, with a shrug of his shoulders, declare, "I made a mistake." He repeatedly engaged in this dance. Every author makes mistakes, but this, we pointed out to the court, was different. Rather than move, as genuine mistakes do, in numerous directions, Irving's so-called mistakes *always* moved in one direction: denial of the Holocaust, exonerations of the Third Reich, and implication of the Jews. As these putative mistakes piled up, it became clear to all—except possibly to Irving—that they were hardly inadvertent. It certainly was evident to Judge Gray, who, in his lengthy judgment, declared that Irving's "falsification of the historical record was deliberate." So, too, with Eichmann. The more Eichmann piled one excuse on top of another—"it was a mistake," "this is a forgery," or "this is the work of a sloppy bureaucrat"—the more he sounded like a drowning man grasping at straws, and the more it must have been clear to the judges that this man would say anything if he thought it would clear him.

Hausner kept the pressure on. One document spoke of Eichmann as "the person who could have given me details about the persecution of the Jews." Yet another mentioned, "There was a special apparatus for all extermination . . . matters. . . . And the Chief of the operation was SS Obersturmführer Eichmann." Finally, after having laid out an array of such documents in which high-ranking Nazis referred to his "special assignment" regarding Jewish matters, Hausner asked whether these high-ranking Nazi officials "are all lying and only you are telling the truth." Eichmann's response—"I am basing myself on the documents"— sounded rather unpersuasive. Hausner scored again when he challenged Eichmann's claim that his subordinates stationed in other countries took their orders from the German officials there. Eichmann contended that if they did have a hand in murderous activities, responsibility rested with their superiors in the particular country, and not with him. Why, then, Hausner wondered, had he referred in various documents to "my office in Paris," "my office in Oslo," and, regarding The Hague, "my office"? Why, Hausner asked, all these "my office"s if he did not decide anything? With that simple exchange, yet another of Eichmann's claims collapsed.[18]

Without digressing or engaging in histrionics, Hausner kept the interrogation moving at a steady pace. In September 1943, the Foreign Office asked Eichmann about the status of a Jewish woman then interned in the Netherlands. She was married to an Italian Catholic, and the Italians wanted her returned to Italy. Eichmann responded that, given Italy's recent withdrawal from the war, there was no reason to agree. "I have therefore instructed my office in The Hague to transfer the Simons woman immediately to the East." Hausner observed that Eichmann had simply been asked about her status. Yet he had responded by having her deported. Hausner next took note of the dissonance between Eichmann's claim that he was an officer of low rank, and a 1942 request by SS officials in Paris that he "induce" the Wehrmacht's High Command to instruct its officers in France to supply army escorts for deportations. Why would SS officials assume that he could influence high-ranking army officers? What, Hausner asked, did that have to do with you? Eichmann began a discourse on the French deportations. Hausner cut him off. "But why to you?" Eichmann claimed they had asked him because it was a "transport matter." Yet, Hausner reminded him, he had earlier denied any connection to the escorts who accompanied the deportations. Why did they come to him? "Why you of all persons?" Hausner offered yet another example that seemed to belie Eichmann's claims of lowly status. At the end of September 1943, the Foreign Office approached him regarding the refusal of the senior commander of German forces in Denmark to permit his forces to assist in operations against Jews. (The reasons for his stance are open to some debate.) Hausner, clearly aware that he was drawing blood, asked, "How did you influence the High Command of the Armed Forces?" In Belgium, the military governor, an army officer who disliked Nazi extremism, initially refused to introduce the obligatory wearing of the Jewish badge. Eichmann was instructed to break down the military governor's opposition. How, Hausner asked, did he "get the military to bend, to go along with you?"[19] Eichmann's answers were all variations on a theme: *I was just passing along requests.* The more he repeated it, the less persuasive it sounded, and the less he looked like a low-level bureaucrat.

Finally, Hausner turned to Hungary. In light of Eichmann's denial of having devised the foot marches from Budapest, whose horrific condition dismayed even high-ranking Nazis, Hausner asked him to explain a note he had written on one of the edited pages of the Sassen tapes: "In accordance with my proposal . . . I had them march from Budapest to the Lower Austrian border on a foot march." Unable to explain away this clear-cut statement, Eichmann insisted that he had handled only the technical aspects of the march. Continuing to draw on Eichmann's edits from the Sassen transcripts, Hausner read Eichmann's gleeful boasts about how well the deportations went in Hungary, and how the "Hungarian Government set such a pace!" He had told Sassen that, even when the Allies bombed the railway stations "to smithereens," he had remained resolved to "show my iron fist to the Allies," and that, despite the Allies' attempt to "destroy the lines of communication to the Reich and bomb them to pieces," he remained resolved to "still march" the Jews.[20]

Hausner's cross-examination lasted two weeks. Again, some observers contended that, because Hausner never got Eichmann to specifically and unambiguously acknowledge his guilt, Eichmann "won on points." But even if an unequivocal admission of guilt might have provided some observers with psychic satisfaction, on a forensic level it was of limited value. How significant would an admission of guilt be, coming from a man who had willingly participated in a murder program, then claimed he was not responsible because he was following orders, and then subsequently lied about what he did? Despite sometimes badgering Eichmann in a clumsy and inelegant fashion, and holding him responsible for acts to which he was not connected, Hausner had presented an overwhelming body of incriminating evidence to prove that Eichmann's excuses were shams. He demonstrated that Eichmann had a very good memory: he remembered his salary when he trained at Dachau; he recalled the special brandy a colleague had served him; even his own lawyer marveled that he remembered what he had eaten at a 1934 SS dinner—but not the number of Jews he'd forced into deportation trains.[21]

Hausner's "failure" to get Eichmann to admit his guilt reminded me, yet again, of what happened during my legal battle. Before the trial, many people expressed the hope that my lawyers would get David Irving to acknowledge that his claims about the Holocaust were lies. I told one such person that I did not anticipate Irving would fall on his sword in such a fashion. Moreover, I added, startling him a bit, I didn't think it mattered. What value was there to an admission from a man who so consistently manipulated and lied about evidence? Expressions of contrition from people who brazenly lie even when confronted by evidence to the contrary are of limited value. Today they might admit their guilt. Tomorrow they might deny it. And on the next day they might redefine their retraction. Comparisons between these two men are, of course, limited. It is one thing to trample on the truth, and quite another to trample on human lives as Eichmann did. Yet, ultimately, there is a link between those who perpetrated these horrors and those who deny them. One of the first things that became clear to me as I immersed myself in the sewer that is denial was that, even though according to deniers' absurd logic, the Holocaust is a myth, the Jews' nefarious behavior made them nevertheless deserving of being destroyed. In short, it did not happen, but the Nazis would have been justified if they had made it happen. During my trial, David Irving's historical lies and distortions shocked me less than the delight he seemed to take in denigrating, attacking, and ridiculing Jews. The indispensable element of the ideology of both perpetrators *and* deniers is a deep-seated Jew hatred. Not all expressions of anti-Semitism are the same, but these two men seemed to me to share a similar worldview.

The criticisms of Hausner's courtroom tactics were not unjustified. In his memoir, Hausner insisted that his objective had been neither to deliver a "crushing blow" nor to conduct a "show," but to build an airtight forensic argument. However, his behavior during the trial suggests otherwise.[22] Often during his cross-examination he seemed intent on trying to extract that unambiguous confession which, after the trial, he insisted he was not seeking. He seemed to want it, not for the judges, but for an audience that extended well beyond the public gallery. He badgered Eichmann long after having proved his point. It is unclear whether he was emotionally overwrought or playing to the galleries. In either case this behavior was ultimately not just to his own detriment but also to that of this legal proceeding. In the words of the *New York Times*, Hausner's "shrillness and posturing" often obscured his questions and made Eichmann look like a "clever and wily opponent." At moments such as these, the trial became a "prolonged nightmare."[23] He also transformed Eichmann from the low-level bureaucrat who played an exceptionally significant role in the Final Solution into *the* man at the heart of the operation, which he was not. When he did precisely what a prosecutor should do—box Eichmann into a corner from which the only escape was to pile excuse on top of excuse—he performed more than admirably. It was then that he left Eichmann twisting in the wind. When he shouted, hectored, gestured wildly, and kept harping on the same point, he looked more than theatrical; he looked as if he had been bested.

Even if Hausner had not engaged in these theatrics, on some level it is doubtful whether he could have succeeded at the task he had taken upon himself. He wanted to present Eichmann to the world as the epitome of both the literal and the symbolic Nazi, and, in the course of so doing, to take on history itself: to paint an all-encompassing portrait of this man's crimes against a background of German collusion at every level of society, an innate age-old Christian anti-Semitism, and the horrors of a bureaucratic system that made murder a *desideratum*. He wanted to shine the spotlight on Eichmann while simultaneously calling to account a world that silently acquiesced to the horrors under way. It was an inherently impossible task.

After Hausner completed his cross-examination, it was the judges' turn to query Eichmann. According to Israeli judicial procedure, this process is designed to ensure that the judges properly understand the defendant's testimony.[24] Holocaust scholar Omer Bartov aptly describes these exchanges as among "the most fascinating documents about the Holocaust in existence." Judge Raveh, who was the first one to question Eichmann, began with something that sounded surrealistic: a discussion of Immanuel Kant's categorical imperative. Eichmann had told Captain Less that he structured his life on Kant's belief that people must behave so that their actions can be raised to the level of general legislation. In what Gouri described as an "academic debate in a slaughterhouse," Judge Raveh began by asking how Eichmann could mesh his insistence that he lived according to that credo with his actions during the war. Eichmann admitted that during the Final Solution he could not "live entirely according to it, although I would like to do so." Instead, he had to follow the "orders by a supreme head of state." When, Raveh wondered, did he become aware that he could not live according to this principle? Eichmann recalled the first time he had witnessed mass shootings. That was when he knew. Many years later, Servatius's assistant Dieter Wechtenbruch described this to Yablonka as the most "classic truth of intent" he had ever witnessed in a courtroom. Eichmann had acknowledged that he understood the implications of what he was doing but continued to obey his orders nonetheless. Raveh then turned to the statement Eichmann had written while in prison prior to the trial. He had summarized the speech he gave to his men as the Third Reich was crumbling around them: "For five years millions of enemies had assailed Germany, and millions of enemies have been killed. And I estimate that war has cost five million Jews." Eichmann proclaimed that he would jump into his grave fulfilled at having been part of this effort. David Cesarani, in his important study of Eichmann's career, considers this the crucial moment. His moral reflections regarding Kant bore no relationship to his utter contentment—if not joy—at having brought about the death of millions of Jews.[25]

Raveh asked Eichmann about the phrase in the minutes of the Wannsee Conference: "The various types of possible solutions were discussed." "What," he asked, "was talked about there?" Eichmann's answer, delivered in precisely the fashion he had refused to use with Hausner, was short and direct: "The various possibilities for killing." Raveh, turning to the celebratory fireside Cognac chat, asked: "So why was Eichmann included?" Eichmann tried to explain how he came to be there: "Because—we had only just been left alone, and no one else was there, and then Heydrich said how he wanted the minutes to be drafted, and after he listed these items, there was no further talk of these matters. Instead I was asked to drink a glass or two or three of cognac. That is how it happened." Armed with these "relevant instructions," he wrote up the minutes of the meeting at which the process for killing European Jewry had been decided upon. Even twenty years later, he seemed intent on showing that he had followed his orders in a precise fashion.[26]

Halevi began by urging Eichmann to drop his objections to allowing the transcripts of the Sassen interview to be introduced. Halevi was suggesting to Eichmann that, given that his fate was all but sealed, he should let the full truth be heard in the courtroom. "This is likely to be the only public opportunity you will have of showing the world . . . what sort of a man you are, whether . . . you want to evade the truth." Pushing harder, he reminded Eichmann that he had insisted that "an oath is one of the highest moral obligations." Now was his opportunity to fulfill the oath he had freely given at the start of the trial to tell the truth. Eichmann did not budge. Halevi gave up and returned to the topic Hausner had so assiduously tried to keep out of the trial. As he had with Raveh, Eichmann responded directly.

> Halevi: The Jewish functionaries were given duties . . . which greatly facilitated emigration. . . .
>
> Eichmann: Yes sir.
>
> Halevi: And then that could be switched very rapidly and simply to deportation.
>
> Eichmann: Yes sir.
>
> Halevi: [In] Poland . . . Hungary . . . in Amsterdam . . .
>
> Eichmann: Yes.
>
> Halevi: As instruments of German policy regarding

the Jews, these Jewish Councils—shall we say—
considerably facilitated the implementation of mea-
sures against the Jews?

Eichmann: Yes.

Halevi: And saved a great deal of manpower and staff.

Eichmann: Yes.

Halevi: That made it possible, by misleading the victims, to facilitate the work, and also to harness the
Jews themselves to work for their own destruction.

With this exchange, Judge Halevi ensured that the difficult and painful topic of the Jewish Councils—those who, as
he had ruled in the Kasztner trial, had "sold" their souls "to
the devil"—was part of this proceeding. Halevi had previously thwarted Hausner, but never so pointedly and unambiguously. And though this trial had been, for the most part,
exactly what Hausner wanted it to be, a trial of the perpetrators, as it neared its end Judge Benjamin Halevi, with the
cooperation of Adolf Eichmann, called the victims to
account.

Halevi then returned to Eichmann's behavior. He recalled
Eichmann's comment to a colleague who wished to exempt
some Jews from deportation. Exceptions to the rule were
impossible, because they could snowball and the "whole
operation could collapse." However, Halevi observed, Eichmann *had* made exceptions: in Hungary, Jewish Council
members could ask him to exempt their closest relatives.
Eichmann had arranged for the Kasztner train. Eichmann,
knowing that he could not claim credit for this and still hold

to his "only following orders" defense, protested that his superiors had authorized all such exceptions.

Then, seeming to abandon this line of questioning, Halevi asked rather matter-of-factly: "Personally, you were not an anti-Semite?" Eichmann answered with a simple "No." Halevi observed that some of Eichmann's relatives had married Jews, and that he had a Jewish aunt, Dorczi, whose daughter was categorized as half Jewish by the Nuremberg Laws. Yet he had approved her immigration to Switzerland. In addition, he had helped a Viennese couple escape. "Of course I authorized this. . . . I had no innate hatred of Jews." Eichmann then volunteered, as if to gain the judges' approval, that these "were not the only cases" in which he had helped Jews. After all, he told Halevi, "in every law there were certain loopholes." With that statement Eichmann revealed the stunning inconsistency of his defense. Halevi, without losing a second, bore in with rapierlike directness. At times Eichmann could turn "a blind eye," ignore his oath, and "act according to your human impulses?" Eichmann, apparently aware that he had en-trapped himself, protested rather lamely, "There were a very few cases." Halevi assured him that there was no "need for you to apologize . . . for the fact of the matter is that in a few cases you did something." Then Halevi cut to the heart of the matter. In these cases "you were not so strict about your oath of allegiance?"[27] With that exchange, anything that remained of Eichmann's defense after Raveh's questions totally collapsed. He had known he was doing something wrong, yet he continued to do it. His loyalty oath was not inviolate—it could be abrogated. When he wished, he could abide by the categorical imperative and rescue lives.

Finally, it was Landau's turn. Not surprisingly, given his exchange with Raveh and Halevi, Eichmann now seemed "guarded, vigilant."[28] Landau asked about his statement that he had seen Jews loaded onto freight cars. Eichmann fell back on his faulty-memory excuse: "Jews being loaded onto freight cars? I cannot remember this however hard I think things over." A coolly skeptical Landau made it clear that Eichmann's memory lapse only made him look more complicit: "This is something which, I would assume, no one who had observed it can ever forget." When Landau asked about his role in "forced emigration," Eichmann again claimed that he had worked with "harassed and oppressed" Jews on an "equal footing" in order to "make the best of the muddle." Once again, Eichmann spoke as if this "muddle" was a force of nature and not something caused by the very system he had facilitated.

One of the most compelling moments in his exchange with Landau came when the judge turned to the Wannsee Conference. Intent on verifying the details of precisely what was discussed at the meeting, Landau asked why the specific "methods of killing" were not included in the minutes. Eichmann reminded Landau that Heydrich had given him precise instructions on what was to be included and what was to be omitted. Landau assumed that details of the specific killing methods, such as gas, had been omitted because they were "so important" and Heydrich did not want references to them to be widely circulated. Eichmann corrected Landau. "No on the contrary, Your Honor. Heydrich wanted to make sure that the . . . essential points [were] in the record, and the non-essential points were then left out." Landau, who generally showed no emotion, seemed nonplussed at the thought that the means of killing millions of people were not worthy of mention. Ever the professional, he continued with barely a pause, "Does that mean, then, that the methods of killing were [considered] an unimportant topic?" Eichmann's rather nonchalant response still amazes me: "Oh, the *methods* of killing?" Landau had to remind him: "That *is* what we are talking about." No, Eichmann assured him, there was no specific talk of killing methods.[29]

This part of the trial ended with a brief additional cross-examination by Hausner. Hausner had Eichmann read from the transcript of the Sassen tape: "I do a job if I can understand the need for it or the meaning of it, and if I enjoy doing it. [Then] time will just fly by, and that is how it was with the Jews." Eichmann read on in a flat, matter-of-fact manner: "[When] I received orders to proceed . . . against the guest of the host people, I thought this over, and when I recognized the necessity to do so, I carried out these [orders] with the degree of fanaticism one expected of oneself as a National Socialist of long standing." Eichmann protested, rather lamely, that this referred to the period before 1939. Hausner wisely ignored the protest and asked for a final clarification: "So the 'guest' people is the Jewish People and the 'host' are the Germans. Right?" Eichmann's one-word answer—"Yes"—must have sounded to many in the room like an affirmation not just of Zionism, but of the appropriateness of holding the trial in the Jewish state.[30]

A few days later, the court reconvened for the summations. Hausner wove his weeks of evidence into an all-encompassing whole. It was impressive, sweeping, and, as had been the case from the outset, wrong in many respects. Pushing past the evidence, he accused Eichmann of things for which he was not responsible. He painted the Holocaust as a well-organized top-down bureaucratic endeavor, though it had been a far more incremental and sometimes even haphazard operation. Hausner made the man in the glass booth look more mythic than real. Returning to a theme he had articulated in his opening talk, he linked the two Adolfs, Hitler and Eichmann. This turned Eichmann into a caricature, diminished the culpability of Himmler, Müller, Heydrich, and many others, and put the onus on one man. Unable to bring these higher-ranking Nazis to court, Hausner placed their guilt on Eichmann.[31] It may have served Hausner's short-term rhetorical goal, but it did not serve the cause of history.

Servatius's oral summation was more compact. Homing in on the weaknesses in the prosecution's case, he argued that it had not proved that Eichmann was connected to Kristallnacht, the mass shootings in the East, Operation Reinhard (the program to murder much of Polish Jewry), and various other aspects of the Final Solution. Servatius also revisited his original arguments about the legality of the proceeding. This time, however, he displayed a striking tone-deafness. He argued that, since Israel did not exist during the Final Solution, the victims were "foreigners" for whom Israel had no responsibility. Servatius's use of the term "foreigners" was hardly strategic. Pushing further, he dismissed the notion of a Jewish people as a "legal fiction" and described Israel's actions as "interference" by a "third party" with no connection to the matter. Turning to the 1950 Israeli law under which Eichmann was being tried, Servatius argued that its provision rendering membership in the SS, Gestapo, or SD a criminal act was "precisely what Hitler" did to the Jews: declaring them guilty because of the group to which they belonged. Servatius's comparison disregarded many essential facts, primary among them that one had to choose to be a member of the SS, Gestapo, or SD, whereas Jews did not choose to be Jews. Furthermore, membership in these organizations meant complicity in acts of violence against others. Turning to resettlement programs such as Nisko, Servatius compared them to the kind of "exchange of populations" that every government—including Israel—conducts after a war. He argued that Eichmann deserved credit for enabling two-thirds of Austrian Jews to emigrate and Jewish organizations to "renew their activities." He disregarded the terror that gripped Austrian Jewry under Eichmann's administration, and contended that the money Eichmann forced the Jews to leave behind constituted "voluntary contributions."

Turning from the fate of the Jews to Eichmann himself,

Servatius argued that he had taken a loyalty oath and was, therefore, obligated to remain at his post. To have done otherwise would have constituted a "betrayal of comrades." Servatius elided the fact that these comrades were the very people responsible for mass murder. Servatius's strange manner of expression reached its nadir when he described the gassings as actions taken "within the medical sphere." Halevi immediately interrupted to ask if this was a slip of the tongue. Servatius assured him it was not. The object of the gassings, he explained, was "killing, and killing is within the medical sphere." None of the judges said anything, but it is not difficult to imagine their reaction. Servatius concluded by conjuring up the notion of the biblical Jubilee Year, which occurred every forty-nine years, during which prisoners were released. He asked the court, "not to pardon and to forget," but "to heal wounds," by issuing a "Solomonic" judgment that would erase the "blemish" caused by Israel's abduction of Eichmann from Argentina. It was unclear whether his reference to a Solomonic judgment meant splitting the wrongs committed by each side— abduction versus mass murder—or to the wisdom of Solomon.[32]

On the mid-December day when the judges were to issue their judgment, Beit Ha'am was packed. The judgment began with a reaffirmation of what had been evident throughout the trial. The judges' perception of the trial was diametrically opposed to Hausner's and, by extension, Ben-Gurion's. A trial, they unequivocally declared, could not be a "forum for clarification of questions of great import." The questions of great import that they believed did not belong were precisely the matters that Hausner considered fundamental to his case: anti-Semitism, the role of other nations in facilitating the Final Solution, and the Allies' failure to assist the Jews. The court's responsibility, they insisted, was to focus on the defendant's actions and to "entirely eliminate" anything foreign to this process. In what may be the most "controversial" aspect of their ruling, they addressed the testimony of Holocaust survivors "who poured out their hearts as they stood in the witness box." Their testimony would be valuable for historians and researchers, but the judges regarded it "as a by-product of the trial." Having begun with this slap at the prosecution and its forensic strategy, they then addressed Servatius's objections. The Holocaust was not a "new crime which had not hitherto been known," but was a criminal act according to the laws of all civilized nations. This trial could not be said, therefore, to constitute retroactive justice. Eichmann and his compatriots knew their acts were wrong. Otherwise, why would they have tried to "efface the traces" of them? Not surprisingly, they also rejected Servatius's contention that Israel had no link to the victims. The aim of the Final Solution was the destruction of the "entire Jewish people." To argue that there was "no connection" between Jews in Israel and Jews murdered by the Nazis "is like cutting away the roots and branches of a tree and saying to its trunk: I have not hurt you." Had the Gypsies, another group designated for annihilation, reconstituted themselves after the war as a sovereign state, they, too, would have had the "natural right" to punish those who murdered its people.

Turning to the kidnapping, they ruled that Eichmann's rights had not been violated in Argentina, since he never applied for asylum, lived there under an assumed name, and committed crimes that Argentina had condemned. Moreover, even if the kidnappers were judged to have violated Argentina's sovereignty, according to international law the person arrested cannot exploit the irregular circumstances of his apprehension to fight the charges against him. The rights of asylum belong to the country, not the offender.[33]

Eichmann's claims that his efforts in Vienna had been for the "mutual benefit" of Jews and Nazis were contradicted by the "witnesses and the documents." Eichmann's assertion that, had the Madagascar plan "materialized, everything would have been in perfect order to the satisfaction of the Germans and the Jews," was "far from the truth." They ruled that Eichmann's contention that Rademacher had forged the document that contained his comment that the Serbian Jews should be shot "lacked credibility." Had it been a forgery, that would have been uncovered at the time. His claim that he reacted to the failure of the trucks-for-lives negotiation with "sorrow" and "fury and . . . anger" was "sheer hypocrisy," given that while he was negotiating he was deporting Hungarian Jews as quickly as possible.[34] His repeated declaration that all he had done was arrange timetables was thwarted by the evidence, which demonstrated that his office ordered which Jews were deported, when, and how. His task was not just to obtain freight cars, but also "Jews to fill them." During his interrogation, Eichmann had told Less that it was his responsibility to "ensure that the freight cars should be used to their maximum capacity." This, the judges declared, said "everything." He commanded those who rounded up Jews, packed them onto the freight cars, without subsistence for the trip, and ensured that they arrived at the killing places in sufficient numbers so that the extermination equipment would operate at maximum capacity.[35] The court ruled that "the legal and moral responsibility of a person who delivers the victim to his death is . . . no less, and maybe even greater than the liability of the one who does the victim to death." Eichmann's claim that he could ignore an order to permit the emigration of certain Jews from Hungary because it was given orally was, the judges declared, "more damning than a hundred witnesses." The order to annihilate the Jews was also given orally, yet he felt entirely bound by it. He claimed he had no power to act on his own, yet he "ascribed to his own subordinates no small degree of initiative."[36]

The judges were not completely persuaded by Hausner, however. They did not believe that Hausner had conclusively proved that Eichmann murdered the small boy in Budapest. More important, Hausner had not proved that Eichmann was connected to Kristallnact, had helped establish the Reinhard camps (Belzec, Sobibor, and Treblinka), participated in the sterilization program, or arranged the death marches. Though his deportation activities in places such as Vienna, Prague, and Nisko during the early years of the war were brutal, the judges correctly reasoned that Hausner had not proved that they were part of the program to exterminate the Jewish people.[37] Ultimately, they found him guilty of what the evidence could prove and, with but a few exceptions, rarely ventured beyond that.

In the final paragraph of their decision, they addressed Eichmann's character rather than his deeds. He had not offered "truthful evidence, in spite of his repeated declarations that . . . his only desire was to reveal the truth. . . . His entire testimony was nothing but one consistent attempt to deny the truth and to conceal his real share of responsibility." Even as they declared him a liar, they offered a backhanded compliment: "His attempt was not unskillful, due to those qualities which he had shown at the time of his actions—an alert mind; the ability to adapt himself to any difficult situation, cunning and a glib tongue. But he did not have the courage to confess to the truth." On the following day, the court convened so that Eichmann could make a statement. Not surprisingly, he bemoaned his misfortune in having "become entangled in these atrocities." He insisted that "guilt for the mass murders is solely that of political leaders," and, reiterating a theme he had adopted from the outset, declared himself one of "the victims." Rather than a monster, he was "the victim of an error in judgment." In short, he was "being sentenced for the 'deeds of others.' "[38]

The sole matter remaining to be determined was his punishment. When the court reconvened to pass sentence, Judge Landau's opening words offered Eichmann some hope. He noted that the Israeli Penal Code gave courts the option to impose any penalty *up to but not exceeding* the penalty pre-scribed by law. Therefore, despite having found him guilty, the court was not obligated to impose death, even though the law under which he was being tried provided for capital punishment. Landau seemed to suggest that they might have decided to spare Eichmann's life. But this was not the case. Death, though not mandatory, Landau continued, was warranted. With a "deep feeling of the burden of responsi-bility," the judges *chose* to impose it. They were the first judges in Israel's history to do so.[39]

Eichmann immediately appealed to the High Court. In the interim, a vigorous debate erupted over the death sen-tence. Some of Israel's leading scholars, including Martin Buber, Yesayahu Leibowitz, and Gershom Scholem, peti-tioned Israeli president Ben-Zvi to commute the death sen-tence. They were joined by others, including the poet Leah Goldberg, and the artist Yehuda Bacon, who had testified at the trial about being deported to Auschwitz at age four-teen. Professor of philosophy Shmuel Hugo Bergmann, who organized the protest, found Bacon's efforts to spare Eich-mann's life deeply moving. "This was, in my eyes, proof that the Judaism of love and compassion still lived and breathed even after the Holocaust." In addition to the academics and artists, a number of rabbis declared that only a Sanhedrin had the right to impose a death sentence. During the debate, Buber approached Ben-Gurion at a meeting of the Bible-study group in which they participated and asked if he could meet with him in order to argue for the commutation of the death sentence. When the prime minister agreed, Buber offered to come to his office. Ben-Gurion decided that since, at age seventy-five, he was younger than the eighty-four-year-old Buber, he would come to Buber. During their two-hour meeting, the secular Buber cited Hasidic Rabbi Menachem Mendel of Kosov: "What the Torah teaches us is this: none but God can command us to destroy a man." Ben-Gurion, who had strongly opposed including the death penalty in the Israeli Penal Code, was not convinced by these arguments. Nonetheless, he thought enough of them to bring the matter to a Cabinet meeting. The Cabinet rejected awarding clemency. Many Israelis agreed. *Maariv* left no question about its editorial stance: "A pardon for Eichmann? No! Six million times no!" The poet Uri Zvi Greenberg, an Israeli national icon, expressed a similar view when he condemned Buber. "I am not speaking on behalf of the Jewish people and not on behalf of the millions. I am speaking for myself. The murder of my father and my mother is my affair. Buber can waive retribution for his parents' death if they were exterminated by Eichmann, but neither he nor other Bubers can demand amnesty for the murderer of my parents."[40] Eventually President Ben-Zvi rejected Eichmann's appeal for a commutation of the sentence. A gallows mechanism was erected—Israel had none—and on May 31, 1962, precisely two years after his capture, the sentence was carried out. His body was then cremated. A mechanism for cremation had to be jury-rigged, since Israel had none. According to Rafi Eitan, the leader of the abduction team, they used a thirty-inch pipe approximately three meters long with burners on both sides, "something like flamethrowers that ran on gas." The hangman was assigned the task of pushing his body into the oven. He was so nervous that he could not keep his hands from shaking and twice knocked the body off the gurney instead of into the crematory. Ultimately, Eichmann's ashes were scattered in the sea to prevent his burial site from becoming a place of pilgrimage for neo-Nazis and anti-Semites.[41]

The trial had ended. The sentence had been carried out. Representatives of the international media who had been present for select moments of this long saga had departed. But the story was far from over. The debate about Adolf Eichmann and his trial was about to enter a new, far more vigorous, acerbic, and intellectually active phase, one that reverberates to this day.

The cover of the February 16, 1963, *New Yorker* featured an artist's rendering of the recently completed and much-debated Pan Am building looming over the iconic Grand Central Terminal and a beflowered Park Avenue. Inside was the first of a series of five articles by Hannah Arendt on the trial. Eventually published as *Eichmann in Jerusalem: A Report on the Banality of Evil*, they would generate a virulent public debate. Arendt's perspective would be condemned as "tasteless," "wicked," "pervaded by vanity," "inaccurate and curiously unfeeling," "gratuitous and distorted."[1] Oxford historian Hugh Trevor-Roper dismissed her as "arrogant" and her book as filled with "half-truths . . . loaded language and . . . double standards of evidence."[2] Her most extreme critics branded her as "sympathetic" to Eichmann and her writings as "claptrap."[3] Her fans were no less effusive. Stephen Spender, who would become Poet Laureate of the United States, described her work as "brilliant."[4] Former Poet Laureate Robert Lowell deemed it a "masterpiece." Arendt's close friend, the novelist and literary critic Mary McCarthy, proclaimed it "splendid and extraordinary." McCarthy did more than just praise Arendt. She defended Arendt, by categorizing her critics according to their ethnic identity. Describing the attacks as a "pogrom," McCarthy contended that Jews were critical of Arendt. Non-Jews, on the other hand, apparently able to see the bigger picture and to react unemotionally, were favorable. Non-Jews who opposed Arendt were summarily dismissed by McCarthy as "special cases." Dwight MacDonald, a former editor of *Partisan Review* and a *New Yorker* and *Esquire* writer, who declared the book "a masterpiece of historical journalism," joined McCarthy and dubbed the "hostile" reviews an expression of "Jewish patriotism," and the non-Jews who criticized Arendt as "Honorary Semites."[5]

Today the passion has ebbed but echoes of that debate linger. To many people, Arendt was a more central character in the Eichmann story than Eichmann himself. And certainly, from an intellectual perspective, she was. Her book and the controversy it aroused put this trial on the intellectual map. Her perspectives on both perpetrators and victims continue to constitute the prism through which many people's view of the Holocaust is refracted.

Arendt was the product of a highly acculturated upper-class German Jewish family in which, she claimed, the word "Jew" was never spoken. She said that she first encountered the term when children taunted her. A Ph.D. from the University of Heidelberg, where she completed a dissertation on Saint Augustine, she had studied philosophy and Protestant theology. As Bernard Wasserstein notes, during her educational career she was exposed to and absorbed a view of Jewish history that ends shortly after the destruction of the Temple in Jerusalem (70 C.E.) with the rise of Christianity. According to this Weltanschauung, Judaism emerged into a higher and more finely developed form—that is to say, Christianity.[6]

She watched her homeland begin its seamless slide into anti-Semitic totalitarianism. Incarcerated briefly in 1933 for helping Zionists, she fled to Paris. There her Zionism became more pronounced. Working for Youth Aliyah, she helped refugee children reach Palestine. When the Nazis invaded France, she was briefly interned. She obtained an American emergency visa and settled in New York, where she taught at Brooklyn College and wrote for *Aufbau*, a German Jewish newspaper. She fought for the creation of a Jewish army to fight in Europe alongside the Allies. Though many of the supporters of a Jewish army were Zionists, her reasoning was different: "You can only defend yourself as the person you are attacked as." For Jews to defend themselves as Englishmen or Frenchmen, when they were being attacked as Jews, would be to fail to defend themselves.[7] After the war, she became executive director of the Jewish Cultural Reconstruction, which tried to recover the Judaica the Nazis had looted. In 1951, she published *Origins of Totalitarianism*, in which she argued that totalitarian societies, such as the Third Reich, by totally dominating all aspects of an individual's life, are capable of compelling people not only to perform horrific acts, but to perceive them as essential. This book established her academic reputation.

When Israel announced the date for Eichmann's trial, she proposed to *New Yorker* editor William Shawn that she cover it for the magazine. Shawn, who had just published James Baldwin's series on the African American community, accepted readily. For Arendt this was to be both an intellectual and a personal excursion. She considered her presence in Jerusalem as a chance both to validate her theories of totalitarianism and to fulfill "an obligation" that "I owe my past."[8] Her expectation that the trial would illuminate the nature of totalitarianism put her at immediate odds with both Ben-Gurion and Hausner, who were not interested in proving anything about the nature of totalitarian societies. Her perception of what should happen in Jerusalem, like her sense of the Final Solution itself, was diametrically opposed to theirs. She wanted the trial to explicate how these societies succeeded in getting others to do their atrocious biddings, while the prosecution wanted a laserlike focus on Nazi Germany's wrongs against the Jewish people. Moreover, she perceived of the Holocaust not as a crime against the Jews but a "crime against humanity," perpetrated on the Jews. Eichmann, Arendt posited, was not another link in the long line of anti-Semites but someone who participated in a revolutionary new crime. Hausner, as he made clear from the very first paragraph of his speech, believed him to be *the* ultimate link in that chain.

However, it was not just history that separated Arendt from the prosecution. Her view of how the trial should be constructed was as narrow and formalistic as Hausner's was expansive. She believed the trial should be limited to Eichmann's deeds—"not the sufferings of the Jews, not the German people or mankind, not even anti-Semitism and racism." Hausner's decision to give pride of place to the victims, particularly those with no direct connection to Eichmann, infuriated her. She considered most of the witnesses entirely irrelevant. Her view of what the trial should be was far closer to the judges' than Hausner's. Not only did she completely differ with Hausner's forensic premise, but she was incensed by his courtroom style. She grew infuriated as he allowed the witnesses to tell their stories in an unrestrained fashion. She considered the trial a Ben-Gurion–orchestrated and Hausner-executed "mass meeting" designed to affirm Zionist ideology and highlight the notion of *us* (Israelis) versus *them* (the rest of the world).[9]

In her letters from the trial, she voiced a personal disdain for Israel that bordered on anti-Semitism and racism. In a letter to her husband she complained that "honest and clean people were at a premium." She described to her teacher and friend Karl Jaspers the "*peies* [side curl] and caftan Jews, who make life impossible for all reasonable people here." She was full of praise for the judges, but even that contained a note of German Jewish disdain for *Ostjuden*, Eastern European Jews. The judges were "the best of Germany Jewry," whereas Hausner was "a typical Galician Jew. . . . one of those people who don't know any language." (Since he presented his case in multiple languages, she may have meant that his German was not up to her standard.) He spoke "without periods or commas . . . like a diligent schoolboy who wants to show off everything he knows. . . . [He has a] ghetto mentality."[10] She had shown her contempt for East European émigrés and their concerns as early as 1944, when she denigrated the European émigré press in the United States for "worrying their heads off over the pettiest boundary disputes in a

Europe thousands and thousands of miles away—such as whether Teschen belongs to Poland or Czechoslovakia, or Vilna to Lithuania instead of to Poland." As Tony Judt observed, "No '*Ost-Jud*' would have missed the significance of these disputes."[11] Her scorn for Hausner's Eastern European roots are noteworthy given that she had Russian grandparents and her mother spoke German with a thick Russian accent. (It is striking that one of her closest friends, Alfred Kazin, who spent great swaths of time with Arendt and her husband, learned of this only in a 1985 biography.) Her comments about Hausner typified her inclination to adopt, according to Bernard Wasserstein, "the virulent vocabulary and imagery of anti-Semites like Edouard Drumont and J. A. Hobson in denouncing Jewish capitalists."[12]

However, it was Middle Eastern, often called Oriental, Jews who elicited her most acerbic comments. "The country's interest in the trial has been artificially whetted. An oriental mob that would hang around any place where something is going on is hanging around in front of the courthouse." (In another letter, she again used the term "oriental mob." It was clearly not a slip.) She felt as if she were in "Istanbul or some other half-Asiatic country." She showed particular contempt for the Israeli police, many of whom were of Middle Eastern origin. "Everything is organized by a police force that gives me the creeps, speaks only Hebrew and looks Arabic. Some downright brutal types among them. They would obey any order."[13] Such a comment by Arendt, who believed this trial was about obeying orders, gives one pause. Her critic and longtime friend, the great scholar of Jewish mysticism Gershom Scholem would accuse her of "suffering from a lack of *ahavat Yisrael*," love of the Jewish people.[14] Had he known of these comments, he might have accused her of far more. Even the fact that the trial was being conducted in Hebrew, Israel's official language and one she had trouble learning, irked her.[15] She described the "comedy of speaking Hebrew when everyone involved knows German and thinks in German."[16]

Her critique of Israel spilled over into her analysis of aspects of the trial. At one point, Hausner mentioned the 1935 Nuremberg Laws, which prohibited marriages between Jews and "Aryans." Arendt described his references to the law as "breathtaking" in both "irony" and "naïveté" because, she claimed, Israel had a similar law. How could the attorney general criticize Nazi Germany when Israel also banned such marriages? Arendt overstated the case. There is no Israeli agency empowered to perform *civil* marriages, even those between coreligionists of any faith. However, any marriage performed elsewhere, including a mixed marriage, is fully legal and is recognized as such by the Israeli government. (The fact that there is no civil authority in Israel that can perform marriages rightfully upsets many Israelis, as does the exclusive power the Orthodox rabbinate has in relation to Jewish marriages.[17])

While these comments about Israelis are troubling, it was her evaluation of the relationship between the victims and the perpetrators that unleashed the avalanche of criticism. Where others saw Nazi intimidation of the Jewish leaders, she saw cooperation, if not collaboration. Whereas her critics saw one side holding all the cards and the other with none, she saw a level playing field. Her critique began with the Zionists. Arendt argued that the Nazis considered Zionists "decent" Jews because, in contrast to assimilated Jews, they thought in "national" terms. Without providing any data to justify her accusation, she charged that Zionists "spoke a language not totally different from that of Eichmann." Accepting at full face value Eichmann's protestation that his lifelong dream was to put land "under the feet of the Jews," she described him as a Zionist. She asserted that his idea for settlements in Nisko and Madagascar were evidence of the Nazi regime's "pro-Zionist policy." She seemed to fail to consider the fact that the Third Reich was unequivocally opposed to the creation of an independent Jewish state and that the settlements envisioned by Eichmann and his cohorts would have been draconian police states in which the inhabitants would have been exterminated by "natural" means.

She considered the 1933 Ha'avara Agreement between the German and the Zionists an act of collaboration. As a means of enriching their own coffers and making life miserable for Jews, the Nazis blocked the funds of those Jews planning to emigrate. Most Jews could not get even a small portion of their assets out of Germany. (This is one of the enduring ironies of Nazi anti-Semitic policy. During the initial years of the Nazi regime, Reich policy was to get Jews to emigrate. Yet the Nazis placed numerous obstacles in the Jews' path, often making it impossible for them to do so.) The Ha'avara Agreement allowed Jews immigrating to Palestine to transfer a portion of these blocked funds to the Zionist organization. The organization, in turn, bought German goods that were needed by the Palestinian Jewish community. When the émigrés arrived in Palestine, they received credit for their funds. This distasteful boycott-breaking arrangement was an effort to help Jews salvage some of their savings while developing the Yishuv's infrastructure. At the same time, it worked to the Germans' advantage by creating a market for German goods.[18] However, it was hardly a form of collaboration. As with all other forms of negotiations Jewish groups had with the Reich during this period, the other side held all the cards.

But her critique of the relationship between Nazis and Jews reached its pinnacle in her attack on the Jewish Councils. She held them responsible for the death of millions, contending that, "if the Jewish people had been really unorganized and leaderless, there would have been chaos and misery but the total number of victims would hardly have been between four and a half and six million people." According to her, their "pathetic and sordid" behavior was the "darkest chapter" of the Holocaust. For her, it was darker than the mass shootings and the gas chambers, because it showed how the Germans could turn victim against victim. There are many problems with her argument. She ignored the fact that the Einsatzgruppen murdered tens of thousands of Jews during the first months after their entry into the eastern territories in the summer of 1941 without Jewish councils or community leaders serving, in her words, as "instruments of murder."[19] She not only ascribed to the councils more power than they had, but depicted thousands of council members with the same broad ahistorical brush. Some members acted heroically and some contemptuously. Some preserved lives, others worried only about their own. Some combined these traits. Chaim Rumkowski, leader of the Łodź Judenrat, enjoyed a surfeit of material comforts while ghetto inhabitants starved. Showing megalomaniacal tendencies, he printed postage stamps embossed with his image and ordered the composition of odes of praise to him. He was convinced he could save the ghetto by transforming it into a vital economic resource that the Germans would be loath to destroy. When the Germans wanted to deport Jews, he gave up the elderly and demanded that parents surrender their children. Only workers were protected.

> Brothers and sisters, give them to me! Fathers and mothers, give me your children. . . . I must cut off limbs in order to save the body! I must take away children, and if I do not, others too will be taken, God forbid . . . (terrible wailing). . . . Common sense requires us to know that those must be saved who can be saved and who have a chance of being saved and not those whom there is no chance to save in any case. . . .[20]

Though he is personally reviled, his plan almost succeeded. In August 1944, long after every ghetto had been liquidated, the Łodź Ghetto held thousands of Jews. With defeat in the offing, the Germans shipped them to Auschwitz. Had Soviet forces reached the city a bit earlier, Rumkowski *might* be lauded, not reviled. (During the final deportations, Rumkowski, who had become so habituated to obeying German orders, demanded that ghetto inhabitants obey German orders.) The ambiguity about this man was revealed to me early in my career, when I met a survivor of Łódź who told me where she had been. With a know-it-all cockiness all too symptomatic of young scholars, I contemptuously intoned, "Ah, Łódź. Rumkowski," as if nothing more needed to be said. With an unvarnished rebuke, she declared: "By me he is a hero. I am alive because of him." I was silent.

Arendt's anger about the Judenrat issue was certainly exacerbated by what she considered the prosecution's staged silence on the topic. She believed that Hausner was avoiding the issue because of Ben-Gurion's desire not "to embarrass the Adenauer administration." It is unclear, if not illogical, why Adenauer would have been embarrassed by this topic. The notion of Jewish "cooperation" would probably have been most comforting to many Germans: it might have soothed their consciences by suggesting that the victims were complicit in their own murder.[21] Hausner did consciously avoid the topic because, unlike the Kasztner trial, this was to be a trial of the perpetrators, not the victims.

The members of the Judenrat were not the only Jews Arendt condemned. She also took aim at the Sonderkommandos, those Jews selected to work in the gas chambers. Their job was to deceive the victims before the gassing, so that they would go more submissively to the gas chambers. Before cremating the bodies, they checked their teeth for gold fillings and bodily orifices for sequestered valuables.

Arendt described them as doing "the actual work of killing," but somewhat cavalierly dismissed this as "no moral problem," because, she declared with no historical proof, the SS chose "the criminal elements" for the job. Some indeed were criminals. Many were not. Arendt also failed to mention that they all would be dispatched to the gas chambers every few months, because they knew too much. A new group would replace them, until it, too, was sent to death. Italian Auschwitz survivor Primo Levi offered a radically different assessment of Sonderkommandos, whom he, unlike Arendt, actually encountered in Auschwitz. His words penned in 1986 may have been written for her:

> No one is authorized to judge them, not even those who lived through the experience of the Lager and even less those who did not live through it. I would invite anyone who dares pass judgment to . . . imagine, if he can, that he has lived for months or years in a ghetto, tormented by chronic hunger, fatigue, promiscuity and humiliation; that he has seen die around him, one by one, his beloved; that he is cut off from the world, unable to receive or transmit news; that finally he is loaded on to a train, eighty or a hundred persons to a boxcar; that he travels towards the unknown, blindly, for sleepless days and nights; and that he is thrown at last inside the walls of an indecipherable inferno.[22]

Arendt was also wrong in the case of Yehiel Dinur, Auschwitz survivor and author of popular novels on the

Holocaust. (Arendt justifiably considered his work border-line pornographic.) He asked the court's permission to testify using his pen name, Ka-Tzetnik, an inhabitant of the *Konzentrationslager* (concentration camp), but the court refused. As soon as he entered the witness box, he launched into a description of "the planet of Auschwitz. . . . The inhabitants . . . had no names. . . . They did not dress as we dress here." Arendt believed that Dinur had insisted on testifying and Hausner had accepted even though Dinur had no connection to Eichmann. She fumed at his lyrical testimony. Dinur, she charged, could not distinguish "between things that had happened to the storyteller more than sixteen . . . years ago, and what he had read and heard and imagined in the meantime." She legitimately found it hard to abide his mythologizing of the Holocaust in lieu of testimony. Even Hausner recognized that Dinur's metaphor-laden narrative would not please the court. The prosecutor rather demurely asked Dinur if he might "perhaps put a few questions to you, if you will consent?" Ignoring him, Dinur simply plowed on. When an impatient Judge Landau intervened to ask some questions, Dinur collapsed. Arendt described the moment:

> [H]e started off, as he had done at many of his public appearances, with an explanation of his adopted name. . . . He continued with a little excursion into astrology. . . . When he arrived at "the unnatural power above Nature" which had sustained him . . . even Mr. Hausner felt that something had to be done about this

"testimony" and very timidly, very politely, interrupted. . . . Whereupon the presiding judge saw his
chance as well. . . . In response, the disappointed witness, probably deeply wounded, fainted and answered
no more questions.

Contrary to what Arendt believed, Dinur had not volunteered: Hausner had pressured him to testify. Furthermore,
he had actually met Eichmann, making his testimony relevant even according to Arendt's limited scope for the trial.
Dinur had a South American passport, which he took
to Gestapo headquarters. Eichmann, who happened to be
there, took the passport, tore it into little pieces, threw it in
the garbage, and then mockingly asked, "Are you still a for-
eigner?"[23] Finally, he did not just faint but fell into a deep
coma, a fact reported in the Israeli press.

She was even more contemptuous of Rabbi Leo Baeck, the
revered leader of German Liberal Judaism. Reluctant to
abandon his flock, Baeck shunned multiple opportunities to
emigrate. Imprisoned in Theresienstadt, he did not inform
Jews there who volunteered for deportation that this meant
an almost certain death. He feared that such knowledge
would have rendered their last hours unbearable. Baeck was
so pervasively attached to the idea of order that he may have
been unable to fathom that Jews might somehow resist. He
had, after all, asked the officers who came to deport him to
wait while he paid his utility bills. Arendt accused him of
compounding his failure to inform the victims of their fate
by having the deportations organized by the Jewish police-

men because "he assumed that they would be 'more gentle and helpful' and would 'make the ordeal easier.' " In fact, Arendt posits they were often more brutal and corruptible, because "so much more was at stake for them." (Though the Jewish police were often quite brutal, it is hard to imagine that they were *more* brutal than SS men.)

In *The New Yorker* she described Baeck, whom she met in 1945 in New York when she attended a dinner party in his honor, as being, "in the eyes of both Jews and Gentiles, the 'Jewish Führer.' " There are legitimate grounds to question Baeck's decisions, which denied the victims a chance to rise up, escape, or take some other action. However, Arendt's description of him echoed the language of the enemy and suggested—whether she intended it or not—a siding with the Nazis. However, it did more than just that. It also came close to constituting plagiarism. Raul Hilberg had used this term to describe Baeck in his magnum opus, *The Destruction of European Jews.* He, however, was quoting "one of Eichmann's people," who coined the title for Baeck. In the first edition of her book, Arendt retained the phrase. In subsequent editions, she dropped it. This was one of her only concessions to her critics.[24]

She was incensed when critics accused her of closing the gap between perpetrator and victim. However, sometimes it is hard not to interpret her statements as doing precisely that—such as when she wrote that the "majority of Jews inevitably found themselves confronted with two enemies— the Nazi authorities and the Jewish authorities." She excoriated Hausner for asking witnesses why they did not resist.

Yet her description of Jews going to their death with "sub-missive meekness," "arriving on time at the transportation points, walking on their own feet to the places of execution, digging their own graves, undressing and making neat piles of their clothing, and lying down side by side to be shot" is riddled with the same contempt that she claimed Hausner showed for the victims. In an expression of her deep-seated ambivalence about the trial, she twice described the trial as a "court of the victors."[25]

Though she correctly deduced that, contrary to Haus-ner's exaggerated claims, Eichmann was not the linchpin of the Final Solution, she veered in the opposite direction. Using her *Origins* thesis as a context, she declared him a desk-level bureaucrat who showed little initiative and had few talents. (Hausner also called him a desk killer, but one possessed of great initiative and talents.) "Everybody could see that this man was not a 'monster,' but it was difficult indeed not to suspect that he was a clown." She may well have reached this conclusion before coming to Jerusalem. Prior to the trial, she wrote that she did not want to miss the opportunity to analyze "this walking disaster face to face in all his bizarre vacuousness."[26] She concluded that he showed no "fanatical anti-Semitism" and did not have an "insane hatred" of Jews. He exemplified the "banality of evil," in which normal bureaucrats were simply unaware of the evil that they were doing. His seemingly out-of-touch comments—the train could hold three hundred extra Jews because they did not have luggage, he should have arrested a rabbi rather than try to hire one, and his horror that Less's father was deported—led her to conclude that he could not "think"—that is to say, understand how he sounded to others. She failed to explain why, if Eichmann was unaware that what he was doing was wrong, he and other Nazi officials labored to destroy the evidence. Surely Arendt knew that Eichmann and his cohorts were aware of opposition to the Final Solution. Eichmann received communiqués from the Foreign Office relaying other governments' distress at what was being done to their Jewish citizens. The only way she could have concluded that Eichmann was unaware was to give more credence to his demeanor and testimony at the trial than to what he actually did during the war. His words seemed to hold more sway with her than those of the victims. The memoir released by Israel for use in my trial reveals the degree to which Arendt was wrong about Eichmann. It is permeated with expressions of support for and full comprehension of Nazi ideology. He was no clerk. This was a well-read man who accepted and espoused the idea of racial purity.

Yet there is another side to Arendt's analysis, one that has been unduly ignored by her critics. Her evaluation of the trial is actually more complex than those who have vilified her would acknowledge. Lost in the furor was the fact that not only did she and her most ardent critics share certain opinions, but that she powerfully articulated some of the most basic lessons of this horrific moment in history.

Though she was castigated as being anti-Israel, she believed that Israel was justified in kidnapping Eichmann, since there was no alternative route to bring him to justice.

She supported holding the trial in Israel, the "country in which the injured parties and those who happened to survive are." When Karl Jaspers disagreed, she wrote him a letter that is remarkable for its use of the first person plural. "*We* kidnapped a man who was indicted in the first trial in Nuremberg. . . . *We* abducted him from Argentina because Argentina has the worst possible record for the extradition of war criminals. . . . *We* did not take the man to Germany but to our *own* country." (Emphasis added.)[27] Israel, she insisted, "had as much right to sit in judgment on the crimes committed against their people, as the Poles had to judge crimes committed in Poland." She considered the charge that Jewish judges would be biased "unfounded," wondering why the partiality of Jewish judges should be any more in question than that of the Polish or Czech judges who had presided over war-crimes trials in their countries. She dismissed the contention that, since Israel did not exist at the time of the crime, it did not have jurisdiction, as "legalistic in the extreme," as well as "formalistic [and] out of tune with reality and with all demands that justice must be done." She articulated what Israel's critics ignored: there was no international court to preside, and no other country, Germany included, wanted to host it. For Arendt, having this trial in Israel had profound—if not metahistorical—significance. As she wrote in a too frequently overlooked passage in *Eichmann in Jerusalem:*

[F]or the first time (since the year 70, when Jerusalem was destroyed by the Romans), Jews were able to sit in

judgment on crimes committed against their own people, . . . for the first time they did not need to appeal to
others for protection and justice, or fall back upon the
compromised phraseology of the rights of man—
rights which, as no one knew better than they, were
claimed only by people who were too weak to defend
their [rights] . . . and enforce their own laws.[28]

Ben-Gurion, for whom Israel represented the Jewish emergence from powerlessness, could not have stated matters
more forcefully. Her incisive assessment of the weakened circumstances of those who are forced to rely on the "rights of
man" for their protection should have been welcomed
warmly by any Zionist or, for that matter, by any person
who accurately assessed how Jews had been abandoned by a
so-called Enlightened Europe during World War II.

Arendt's criticism—both public and private—of Israel
was harsh. However, as with so much else she wrote, there is
another side to the story. By the time she came to the trial,
she had already broken with mainstream Zionists. She had
wanted a binational state, opposed Israel's policies toward
its Arab minority, and was troubled by the rigid control of
the country by one party, which was dominated by one man.
However, when the virulently anti-Zionist American Council for Judaism offered her a public forum to answer her critics, she declined, even though other Jewish organizations
were attacking her and encouraging others to do likewise. At
the height of the attacks on her, she wrote to Elmer Berger,
the head of the organization:

You know that I was a Zionist and that my reason for breaking with the Zionist organization was very different from the anti-Zionist stand of the Council: I am not against Israel on principle, I am against certain important Israeli policies. I know . . . that should catastrophe overtake this Jewish state, for whatever reasons . . . this would be the perhaps final catastrophe for the whole Jewish people.[29]

Regarding postwar Germany's attitude toward war criminals, she was often more forthright—honest—about Germany's policies than Ben-Gurion had been. He felt it politically prudent to ignore West Germany's lax attitude toward war criminals. In contrast, Arendt illuminated it. She observed that whereas Israel had to "ferret out criminals and murderers from their hiding places," in Germany the murderers were more than hiding in plain sight, they were "flourishing in the public realm." Those few who were tried received "fantastically lenient" sentences. Adenauer's claim that only a "relatively small percentage" of Germans had been Nazis was a lie. The truth was "the exact opposite." Adenauer's historical revisionism reminded her of Eichmann's. "Eichmann's distortions of reality were horrible because of the horrors they dealt with, but in principle they were not very different from things current in post-Hitler Germany." One of her harshest critics, Norman Podhoretz, described her comments as "perhaps the most severe indictment of Adenauer's Germany that has yet been seen this side of the Iron Curtain."

She also fearlessly condemned the Vatican, which in 1944 joined Roosevelt, Churchill, and others in demanding that Horthy halt the deportations—but with a proviso added by the Papal Nuncio assuring the Hungarians that this protest did not spring from a "false sense of compassion." Arendt describes this noxious phrase as a "lasting monument to what the . . . desire to compromise with the men who preached the gospel of 'ruthless toughness' had done to the mentality of the highest dignitaries of the Church."[30] She was condemned for dismissing the victims' testimony as emotional and out of place in the courtroom, but so did the Israeli judges, who deemed it irrelevant to the legal proceedings. In contrast to Hausner, she considered Eichmann a "tiny cog." However, she thought this was "legally pointless" as a justification for his actions, because "all the cogs in the machinery, no matter how insignificant," were necessary for it to operate.[31] Eichmann's assertion that his only alternative to following orders was to commit suicide was, according to her, a "lie" unsupported by the evidence. SS members, she noted, could "quit their jobs without serious consequences." They might be shamed before their colleagues or sent to the Eastern front, which was no small matter, but they were not killed. That was reserved for the victims. No defendant in a Nazi war-crime trial has documented a single instance in which someone who refused to kill Jews was executed. The classic excuse—"I had no option"—was not true.[32]

Much scorn was heaped on her for supposedly suggesting that the Nazis' evil was "banal." She thought nothing of the kind. She used the term "banal" to bolster her contention that Eichmann did not act out of a deep ideological commitment or because he was inherently evil. Had he acted out of such motivations, his actions would have made "sense." She tried to understand how he, and so many other Germans, so seamlessly became killers. They were seemingly normal people who performed unprecedentedly evil acts. She believed that many of them acted in this fashion even though they were not initially motivated by an irrational, deep-seated hatred. It was the transformation of seemingly normal people into killers that rightfully intrigued her. Though much of what she said about the Jewish victims and the manner in which she said it is disturbing, her contention that many of the perpetrators were not innately monsters or diabolical creatures but "ordinary" people who did monstrous things not only seems accurate but is the accepted understanding among most scholars of the perpetrators. It is precisely their ordinariness—their banality—that makes their horrific actions so troubling. In many respects it is the behavior of these people—and there were hundreds of thousands if not millions of them—that constitutes the unfathomable question at the heart of the Final Solution.

However, in Eichmann's case her analysis seems strangely out of touch with the reality of his historical record. Though he may not have started out as a virulent anti-Semite, he absorbed this ideology early in his career and let it motivate him to such an extent that even well after the war he described for Sassen, the Dutch Nazi who interviewed him in Argentina, the joy he had felt at moving Hungarian Jews to their death at an unprecedented clip and his pleasure at having the death of millions of Jews on his record.

Some of the most powerful moments of her book, for example, her expressions of reverence for those who refused to participate in the killing operation and instead reached out to help Jews, were also lost in the cacophony of criticism. In his testimony, Abba Kovner told the story of Anton Schmidt, a German sergeant, who supplied Jews with money, arms, and forged papers until he was caught and executed. Schmidt received no financial gain. Writing with uncharacteristic emotion, Arendt described the courtroom's reaction:

> [A] hush settled over the courtroom; it was as though the crowd had spontaneously decided to observe the usual two minutes of silence in honor of the man named Anton Schmidt. And in those two minutes, which were like a sudden burst of light in the midst of impenetrable, unfathomable darkness, a single thought stood out clearly, irrefutable, beyond question—how utterly different everything would be today in this courtroom, in Israel, in Germany, in all of Europe, and perhaps in all countries of the world, *if only more such stories could have been told* [emphasis added].

If there are any "lessons" to be gleaned from the Holocaust, this is the central one. She contrasted Eichmann's "I had no choice" with Schmidt's example to the contrary and offered a searing condemnation of her fellow Germans: "Many Germans . . . probably an overwhelming majority of them must have been tempted *not* to murder, *not* to rob, *not* to let their neighbors go off to their doom . . . and not to become accomplices in all these cases by benefitting from them. But, God knows, they had learned how to resist temptation." She linked Anton Schmidt to the Bulgarian government and the Danish people, all of whom refused to comply. Using italics to ensure that her words would literally thunder from the page, she declares that the actions of Schmidt, the Bulgarians, and the Danes demonstrated that, when faced with Nazi-like terror, "most people will comply *but some people will not*." The Final Solution could have *"happen[ed] in most places,"* but, once again Arendt put her words in italics, *"it did not happen everywhere."* Eichmann could have said no but chose otherwise. Arendt invests the dissenters' actions with almost cosmic significance. "Humanly speaking, no more is required and no more can reasonably be asked for this planet to remain a place fit for human habitation." I have read few more eloquent paeans to the small number of individuals who refused to participate in the Holocaust or a more devastating condemnation of those who did.[33] It has joined in my lecture folder the eloquent responses to Hausner's query why they did not resist given by the witness Moshe Beisky, the magistrate who refused to escape because he knew it would mean death to the other eighty men in his barracks, and the witness Ya'akov Gurfein, who after being pushed from a deportation train by his mother made his way through Slovakia, Romania, and Hungary to Palestine. Yet I added Arendt's comments to the folder with some hesitation, for while she had unlimited admiration for non-Jews who acted heroically, she seemed unable to find any Jewish heroes. She did approve of Warsaw Ghetto fighter Zivia Lubetkin-Zuckerman, because her testimony was "free of sentimentality or self-indulgence, her facts well organized, and always quite sure of the point she wished to make."[34] Yet Arendt seemed unmoved by Lubetkin-Zuckerman's record of participating in the first armed uprising against the Nazis *anywhere* in Europe. The ghetto fighters knew that most of them would die. Nonetheless, they fought in order to reclaim Jewish pride. Arendt seemed not to find this worthy of notice.

She supported the death penalty imposed upon Eichmann, though she disagreed with the court's rationale for it. She argued that Eichmann should have been found guilty, not of crimes against the Jewish people, but of crimes against humanity carried out on the body of the Jewish people. She would have had the judges declare:

> Even if eighty million Germanys had done as you did, this would not be an excuse for you. . . . You have carried out . . . a policy of mass murder. . . . And just as you supported and carried out a policy of not wanting to share the earth with the Jewish people and the people of a number of other nations—as though you and your superiors had any right to determine who should and who should not inhabit the world—we find that no one, that is, no member of the human race, can be expected to want to share the earth with you. That is the reason, and the only reason you must hang.

Hardly the words of someone who "defend[ed] Eichmann" or was "pro-Eichmann," as one Jewish newspaper in the United States labeled her.[35]

Arendt's critics ignored her support of Israel's right to judge and to impose the death penalty. With few exceptions, they elided her condemnation of Eichmann's lies, Adenauer's duplicity, the Vatican's ethical compromises, and the failure of most Europeans to aid desperate Jews. They lost sight of her eloquent praise of those who did break with the majority and her citation of them as proof that *something* could have been done. Though she castigated Jews for not resisting, she tempered her critique with the very accurate observation that "no non-Jewish group or people had behaved differently."[36] Her critics castigated her for condemning the Judenräte, but failed to consider that she was not alone in doing so. In fact, some of the most ardent attacks on them came from the victims themselves. In the Warsaw Ghetto, the historian Emanuel Ringelblum, creator of the famed Oyneg Shabes Archive, refused to interact with the Judenrat. Ghetto fighters Yitzhak Zuckerman and Zivia Lubetkin-Zuckerman, and Abba Kovner accused them of betrayal. As we have seen, Halevi clearly felt this way and made sure that the trial addressed the topic. One of the main disruptions of the trial had come when a member of the public began to shout and hurl abuse at a member of the Hungarian Judenrat who was testifying. The spectator accused the witness of being complicit in the murder of his relatives.

Why, then, was her critique singled out? Why did her

critics ignore these aspects of her views? Jews were particularly sensitive to the fact that her platform was *The New Yorker*, which, despite being edited by a Jew, was a publication that then epitomized the Jewish fantasy of the stereotypical dominant culture of white Anglo-Saxon Protestants. Eustace Tilley, the "dandy" who is the magazine's icon, represents everything the stereotypical Jew was not and, try as he or she might, could never be. Arendt claimed that she purposely chose a non-Jewish publication for which to write in order to maintain her "distance," but others considered her to have washed dirty linen in public.[37] There were certainly readers who delighted in such criticism of Jews by a Jew. R. H. Glauber, writing in *The Christian Century*, used her theory both to absolve Christianity for having fostered and legitimized anti-Semitism and to blame the victims. Writing about the "part the Jews played in their own destruction through the willing help they offered the Nazis," Glauber mused, "If Eichmann was guilty . . . are not those Jews also guilty?"[38] Many *Christian Century* readers probably found her insistence that anti-Semitism was not at the heart of the Holocaust particularly appealing. Arendt's comments were embraced by theologians, intellectuals, and humanists, among others, who welcomed a universal explanation for genocide that freed them from having to grapple with the anti-Semitic legacy of a European culture they extolled.

However, it was not just *where* she voiced her comments but *how* she voiced them that aroused such passions. Even her supporters acknowledge that she "bears some of the responsibility for how her book was read (and even misread) and why it caused so much pain and anger." A sympathetic biographer described her as "imperious in tone" and "peculiarly insensitive."[39] Her friend Alfred Kazin, who had covered the trial for *The New Republic*, faulted her for projecting an air of "detachment" when, in actuality, she was "as distraught as the rest of us." In an appreciative essay, Tony Judt described her remarks about Jewish responsibility as "insensitive and excessive."[40] The attacks on her, many of which were over the top, elicited responses from her that were borderline—it's unclear which side—anti-Semitic. In a comment that lends credence to Wasserstein's claim that she absorbed the anti-Semitism of the historians on whose work she depended, she wrote Jaspers, "In the long run it's perhaps beneficial to sweep out a little of that uniquely Jewish rubbish."[41]

Though both her venue and her mode of expression exacerbated the intensity of the attacks on her, it is ultimately *what* she said that caused the storm. She saw symmetry between the Nazis and their victims where there was none. She extolled non-Jewish heroes, like Anton Schmidt, but identified no Jewish ones. She saw Jewish victims—particularly in terms of their response to persecution—as one undifferentiated whole. Ultimately, her accusations were simply not supported by the data. Even some of her defenders had to acknowledge her errors, though they tried to minimize them. John McGowan argued, "Inevitably she got some facts wrong, but none crucial enough to discredit her argument."[42] Hans Mommsen acknowledged, "She frequently relied on insufficient study of the available primary sources to support the far-reaching conclusions she drew."[43] Regarding her comments about the Jewish Councils, Elisabeth Young-Bruehl, with a somewhat greater degree of candor, conceded that her "knowledge of conditions in the Eastern European ghettoes . . . was not always extensive enough to support her generalizations."[44] Young-Bruehl and Mommsen are too kind. McGowan is simply wrong. She got far more than "some facts wrong." The primary source material is far from "insufficient" to support many of her conclusions. It contradicts them. Tens—if not hundreds— of thousands of Soviet Jews were murdered without council leaders designating who was to be taken. There were no Jewish police at Babi Yar. She was particularly wrong regarding Eichmann's role. As Raul Hilberg, on whose work she heavily relied and which she often quoted (but to whom she gave less than proper credit[45]), observed:

> She did not recognize the magnitude of what this man had done with a small staff, overseeing and manipulating Jewish councils in various parts of Europe, Austria, and Bohemia-Moravia, preparing anti-Jewish laws in satellite states, and arranging for the transportation of Jews to shooting sites and death camps. . . . She did not discern the pathways that Eichmann had found in the thicket of the German administrative machine for his unprecedented actions. She did not grasp the dimensions of his deed.[46]

Yaacov Lozowick, who, prior to studying the bureaucrats who carried out the Final Solution, agreed with her thesis, observes that Eichmann and his colleagues were completely cognizant of their crimes. Their only regret was of being caught. Christopher Browning, who relies on her theoretical framework for his analysis of the perpetrators, believes she was "fooled" by Eichmann's courtroom strategy.[47] Michael Marrus, who considers the attacks on her unfair, acknowledges that she had a tendency to "pontificate . . . rather than to muster evidence" and that there were "serious inaccuracies in depicting both the Nazis and their victims."[48] Ironically, in the wake of the debate over her work, Arendt—who had been cavalier with history—called upon historians, reporters, and even poets to "stand guard over the facts."[49]

Even her fans have used her arguments in a questionable fashion. It is hard to imagine that she would have approved of the widely praised putative documentary *The Specialist* by Eyal Sivan and Rony Brauman, even though they credit Arendt as their inspiration. They spliced together different portions of the trial without letting their viewers know that they had done so. They mixed the audio from one portion and the visuals from another. They inserted laughter where there is none. They selectively quoted from witnesses' testimony, thereby distorting the import of their words. In so doing they created scenarios that never occurred. For example, they cited the first portion of Franz Meyer's testimony. He had negotiated with Eichmann in Berlin in the mid-1930s and found that Eichmann had then behaved as a "clerk" or a "bureaucrat" who simply fulfilled his duties. However, they omitted the next sentence in which Meyer described Eichmann's subsequent behavior in Vienna. He acted as an "autocrat controlling life and death, [who] received us impudently and crudely." Since the filmmakers' objective is to portray Eichmann not just as a "clown" and an "everyman," but as someone unfairly prosecuted—if not persecuted—by Israel, including the second portion of Meyer's testimony would have been problematic, though honest, for them. Most reviewers, unaware of the film's creative approach to the facts, took what they saw on the screen as a legitimate portrayal of the trial.[50]

There is another troubling aspect to her report. Many people—both her supporters and her critics—still consider *Eichmann in Jerusalem* as Michael Marrus described it, a "journalistic"—that is, eyewitness—account of Arendt's "overall impression of the trial."[51] They assume it was an eyewitness account because she gave every impression that it was. She begins with the words "Beth Hamishpath," the Israeli equivalent of "Oyez, oyez, oyez," and a detailed description of the courtroom. In a note to the reader she states, "I covered the Eichmann trial at Jerusalem for *The New Yorker.*" She rejected some of the accusations against her by writing, "I would have never gone to Jerusalem if I had shared these views."[52] The eyewitness nature of her report is crucial to her evaluation of the man in the glass booth. "Everybody could see that this man was not a 'monster.'" "The longer one listened to him . . ."[53] But she was not in the courtroom during the most crucial moments of his testimony. In fact, she was absent for much of the trial.

Present when it began on April 11, she was by May 10 vacationing in Basel.[54] She returned five weeks later and heard Servatius examine Eichmann. She left just before Hausner began his cross-examination.[55] Anyone who has witnessed a trial knows that the demeanor of a defendant, particularly in a contentious case such as this, is entirely different when he is being examined by his lawyer from when he is being cross-examined, even more so when that cross-examination is being conducted by a prosecutor intent on proving that he is a murderer of millions. If she had been present when Eichmann was locked in an adversarial exchange with Hausner, might she have gathered some insight from his demeanor and body language? Might she have seen the "passion and rage" described in *France-Soir*? Conversely, had she been absent when Abba Kovner told Anton Schmidt's story, she would not have witnessed the "sudden burst of light" and the way the public paid him tribute.

Zindel Grynszpan, the father of Herschel, the young man whose murder of a German official gave the Nazis the excuse to launch Kristallnacht, testified early in the trial. Seeing his demeanor in the witness box almost made her change her opinion about witnesses.

This story took no more than perhaps ten minutes to tell and when it was over—the senseless, needless destruction of twenty-seven years in less than twenty-four hours—one thought foolishly: Everyone, everyone, should have his day in court. . . . [The] story needed a purity of soul, an unmirrored, unreflected innocence of heart and mind that only the righteous possess. No one either before or after was to equal the shining honesty of Zindel Grynszpan.[56]

Had she only read the transcript of his testimony, would she have felt that "shining honesty"? Writing about much of the trial from transcripts does not, of course, invalidate Arendt's conclusions. Many great trial books have been based solely on transcripts. However, her agency derived, in great measure, from her status as a witness. Her failure to reveal that she was not there for significant portions of the proceedings constituted a breach of faith with readers. One wonders how *The New Yorker*, known for rigorous fact-checking, failed to acknowledge this.

Hannah Arendt spoke with many voices. One modulated itself for the likes of Mary McCarthy and her set, many of whom delighted in and felt liberated by a Jew's severe critique of Ben-Gurion, Israel, and her fellow Jews.[57] Her comments freed them from having to self-censor when they spoke of Jewish matters. This Arendt was flippant, cruel, glib, and got many of her facts wrong. This Arendt may also have been subliminally writing for her teacher and former lover, the revered philosopher Martin Heidegger, who joined the Nazi Party in 1933, ejected Jewish professors from the university where he served as rector, affirmed Nazi ideals, and never recanted his wartime actions. His claim to have embraced Nazism as a means of protecting the university is, at its very best, untrue. In 1960, a few months before the trial, Arendt considered dedicating one of her books to Heidegger but decided not to, because it might upset others. In an unused dedication, she described him as "my trusted friend to whom I have remained faithful and unfaithful." She helped resurrect his postwar career by minimizing his Nazi affiliations and fighting to get him readmitted to the scholarly world. When *Der Spiegel* exposed his wartime record, she protested that people should "leave him in peace."[58] This Arendt was intellectually inconsistent when it served her purposes. She castigated Hausner for not limiting his focus to Eichmann's deeds and introducing all sorts of irrelevant material. Yet, as Leora Bilsky observes, by insisting that the topic of the Judenräte should have been included as a means of demonstrating the victims' complicity, she was guilty of doing precisely what she faulted Hausner for: introducing ancillary topics. Both Hausner and Arendt had extrajuridical agendas for the trial. He acknowledged his (educating Israeli youth and delivering a Zionist message). She failed to acknowledge hers (warning about totalitarian regimes) and brutally castigated Hausner for his.[59]

But Arendt had yet another "voice," one whose cadence was decidedly different from the one she used in her *New Yorker* dispatches and her letters of the time. She began her first lecture in Germany after the war with the statement "I am a German Jew driven from my homeland by the Nazis."[60] This Arendt worried deeply about the security of Israel. After visiting Israel in the wake of the 1967 War, she told Jaspers how "really quite wonderful that an entire nation reacts to a victory like that not by bellowing hurrah but with a real orgy of tourism—everybody had to go to have a look at the newly conquered territory." She seemed to understand the Israeli psyche in a way she had not six years earlier. "As far as the country itself is concerned, one can clearly see from what great fear it has suddenly been freed." She subsequently wrote McCarthy, "Any real catastrophe in Israel would affect me more deeply than anything else." In 1973, during the Yom Kippur War, she lamented the "frightening news from Israel" and the "amount of sheer hatred and the complete isolation" directed at Israel at the UN.[61] These were *not* the words of an enemy of the Jewish state.

Her observations about Grynszpan, Schmidt, and the few Germans who broke with the majority cannot fail to enter the heart and the mind. She correctly deduced that there was something entirely unprecedented about this crime: Germany wanted to wipe out an entire people, leave no witnesses, and cover up the evidence. She understood that this was not simply anti-Semitic persecution of tremendous proportion, and that it therefore deserved special attention and offered important warning signs in a nuclear world that has raised genocide to an almost common occurrence. In fact, today it is a "truism" in precisely those circles from which her critics came that the Holocaust was a crime against the Jews *and* against humanity, and that it constitutes a warning about the possibility of evil. It was an unprecedented crime that far surpassed any preceding act of anti-Semitism. No one had ever tried to annihilate a people and then erase any vestige either of them or of the crime. It was this argument that Holocaust survivors, among others, used to justify a

Holocaust museum adjacent to America's sacred public space, the National Mall, and for London's Imperial War Museum to devote an entire floor to the Holocaust. It was this argument that they used to push for the introduction of the topic into public-school syllabi. This mesh of the particular and the universal has ensured that the Holocaust is "remembered" outside the confines of just the Jewish community. However, it has also allowed people to ignore the obsessive Jew hatred that was at the heart of the Final Solution. Some people mourn the victims yet turn their animus toward the State of Israel in a way that borders on anti-Semitism.

And then there was the Hannah Arendt who seemed unable to acknowledge that the Final Solution, despite its "universal" implications, was not a great rupture in all that had come before, but was the outcome of the anti-Semitism that was scripted culturally and theologically into the bedrock of European culture. Eichmann and his cohorts did not randomly go from being ordinary men to being murders. They traversed a path paved by centuries of pervasive anti-Semitism. They "knew" this road and, given the society in which they lived, it seemed true and natural. Arendt, so deeply and viscerally committed to the European culture that nurtured the animus, seemed unable to acknowledge this reality. Though she protested—methinks a bit too much—that she wrote as the neutral observer, in fact she was torn between the particularism of her Jewish roots and the universalism of the intellectual world to which she was so wedded. (Much of that world was, of course, inhabited by

Jews, who were universalists in a mode unique to Jewish intellectuals.)[62]

She was rightfully criticized for her ahistorical comments about the Judenrat. Yet it must be acknowledged that she raised painful and important questions in relation to leadership and individual responsibility. In notes for a lecture given at Wesleyan before her articles appeared in *The New Yorker*, she wrote, "If you say to yourself in such matters: who am I to judge?—you are already lost."[63] The Judenräte leaders were not the collaborators she paints them to be. They had no cards to play. They lacked the power to halt the Nazis' resolute determination to murder Jews. However, can we afford to shy away from asking if they had the right to arrogate for themselves the choice of victims? Who gave them the authority to withhold crucial information from people who voluntarily boarded deportation trains? Who empowered them to decide who should board those trains? I cannot answer—much less even fully pose—these questions, but Arendt reminds us that they hover in the gray zone.

As a woman—and one cannot deny that some of the passionate fury against her was intensified because she was a woman—with an acerbic mode of expression, Hannah Arendt sometimes seemed more interested in turning a good phrase than on understanding its effect. She wanted to needle her readers to examine their assumptions. Yet, in order to do so, one must write in a manner that will allow one's words to be heard. She was guilty of precisely the same wrong that she derisively ascribed to Adolf Eichmann.

She—the great political philosopher who claimed that careful thought and precise expression were of supreme value—did not "think." She wanted to provoke her readers to re-evaluate their assumptions, but she either did not care or did not fully consider how her caustic comments might be heard by them. Many of the important things she had to say were lost in the din she created with her cruel statements and haphazard treatment of historical data. Ultimately, though she claimed to be shocked and deeply hurt by the wrath she had provoked, she was the author, writ large, of her own misfortune.

On some level, of course, it is ridiculous to speak of "misfortune" in relation to an author whose work has shaped contemporary perceptions of the Final Solution. Yet her work, even as it tried to explain critical aspects of the most extensive genocide in human history, submerged the most fundamental and indispensable element of this event. She ignored the bedrock of the Holocaust: the long, tortured (torturing) history of anti-Semitism. It may have taken German National Socialism to pull from the thick soil of Jew hatred the means to murder millions. However, without a pre-existing animus that was so deeply ingrained in Western culture—both secular and religious, enlightened and unenlightened—the Nazis could never have accomplished what they did. Any attempt to separate anti-Semitism from the ignominious legacy of the Final Solution is to distort historical reality. There was an animus that prompted perpetrators to murder with impunity and bystanders to close their countries' doors to those seeking refuge.

Some people, particularly in the Jewish community, will tell you, year in and year out, that anti-Semitism is always increasing in intensity and danger, and that this year the situation is exponentially worse than during the preceding one. These repeated assessments—it's always terrible, and getting more so—have, until recently, been contradicted by reality. Simply put, they were wrong. In North America and Europe, the pessimists based their claims on minor acts of vandalism and rather inane expressions of anti-Semitism. One cannot dismiss these acts, but they never constituted an existential threat. Sometimes the fear of anti-Semitism has been mobilized to motivate Jews to observe rituals, donate to philanthropic causes, or take a particular political position. As someone who delights in her Jewish identity, I cringed whenever I heard someone suggesting that we should "be," "do," or maintain our Jewish identity because "everyone hates the Jews."

However, in the past decade matters have changed dramatically. With the marked exception of North America, the level of anti-Semitic rhetoric has reached new proportions. Though anti-Semitism still emanates from the far right, its increase is due to an embrace by select portions of the Muslim community and by parts of the left as well. In Iran, the ability of a man who is an overt anti-Semite and Holocaust denier to wreak havoc in the world increases daily. Distasteful and historically absurd comparisons are made between Israelis and Nazis. The existence of this anti-Semitism, while deeply troubling, surprises me far less than that so many people accept it with great equanimity. Jews are often admonished, including by fellow members of their "tribe," for overreacting even when the body blows are real. Gross accusations against Israel—rooted in traditional anti-Semitism, as absurd as the charge that an Israeli medical team went to Haiti after the 2010 earthquake to harvest body parts—are accepted by scholars, journalists, and politicians as matters worthy of investigation. While Holocaust deniers do not surprise me, for they are at heart naught but traditional anti-Semites who have found an attention-grabbing tool, I *am* surprised by the number of serious people who, at least until my trial, thought these anti-Semitic charges should not be taken seriously.

One cannot and should not draw a direct line from Arendt's view of the Eichmann trial to those who berate Jews for making too much of contemporary anti-Semitism. Nor, however, can one dismiss the way in which she so seamlessly elided the ideology that was at the heart of this genocide. She related a version of the Holocaust in which anti-Semitism played a decidedly minor role. Others who have found her work a convenient foil for their own political views have picked up the ball and run with it, some of them in order to justify views she would probably never have condoned.

CONCLUSION

The trial's impact extends far beyond Adolf Eichmann and his nefarious deeds. Some of the changes it wrought emanated directly from the court proceedings; others germinated at the trial but were nourished by subsequent events. Some changes affected the Jewish community; others had a far broader reach. Some were profound; others were stylistic. One of those stylistic changes was the adoption of the term "Holocaust." It had already been used before the trial, including in the official translation of the Israeli Declaration of Independence. However, it was cemented into the lexicon of the non-Hebrew-speaking population when the court translators used it throughout the trial. The trial did not just give a universally accepted name to an event, but greatly accelerated the growth of a field of study. In the wake of the trial, scholars already immersed in researching the Final Solution found a growing audience for their work. More scholars began to explore the topic, thereby accelerating the development of what today we call Holocaust and genocide studies. It also had a significant forensic impact. In the immediate aftermath of the trial, a German Ministry of Justice official, in an oblique reference to his country's anemic record of pursuing the war criminals in its midst, predicted, "An avalanche of prosecutions will now have to follow."[1] Prosecutions did follow, though they can be called an "avalanche" only in contrast to what preceded them. Furthermore, the sentences meted out were often embarrassingly short, given the nature of the crime. The trial was partially responsible for convincing the German government to reverse its opposition to extending the statute of limitations, thereby enabling additional war criminals to be prosecuted.[2] The trial reinforced the notion that there is universal jurisdiction over genocide. Even though legal scholars differ over whether Israel was justified in trying Eichmann, there is now a virtual consensus among democratic states that genocidal killers cannot take refuge behind claims of obedience to superior orders.

The trial either caused or accelerated many changes, but there are certain things it did *not* do, despite being credited for them. In both scholarly and popular circles, some have believed that before the trial the topic of the Holocaust was absent from the Israeli and American agendas. Typical of these claims was Tom Segev's assertion that in Israel, until the trial, there was a "depth of silence" about the Holocaust. When I told various Israeli and American acquaintances that I was working on this book, they echoed that view.[3] Sometimes the popular perception about the break in the silence is tied to both the trial and the 1967 Six-Day War. People argue that the trial unlocked the doors of silence regarding the Holocaust and the Six-Day War threw them open. There is, however, a fundamental problem with all these theories as they apply to Israel, America, and even the European continent. If one looks at the historical record, the notion of a "black hole" about the Holocaust prior to the trial seems to be more imagined than real.[4] In the 1950s in Israel, the Holocaust occupied a prominent place in the national discourse. Memorial books and community records were published in Hebrew and Yiddish. Forests, plaques, and monuments commemorated the victims. In 1956, forty thousand Israelis participated in Holocaust Remembrance Day ceremonies.[5] The Holocaust was also present on Israel's political agenda. In 1950, the Knesset, at the insistence of survivors, passed the law for prosecuting Nazis and their collaborators, the law under which Eichmann was charged. The 1954 Kasztner trial also thrust the topic onto the front page. Kasztner's murder in 1957 revived discussion of aspects of the Final Solution. Throughout the decade, there were spirited legislative discussions about establishing Yom HaShoah. Religious parties wanted to link it to a traditional day of Jewish mourning; secular representatives wanted a "neutral" date. There were even debates about its name. Proposals included "Holocaust and Ghetto Uprising," "Holocaust, Uprising, and Bravery Remembrance Day," and, the one that was finally adopted, "Holocaust and Heroism Day." (It is striking that the stripped-down and unheroic "Holocaust Remembrance Day," as it is known outside of Israel, was not seriously considered.)[6] The creation of Yad Vashem was a matter of contention. Though few objected to a memorial, there were fights, many of which spilled over into the public realm, over whether its purpose was to compile survivor testimonies or to conduct research.[7] Throughout these years, Israelis hotly debated and, on occasion, nearly rioted about accepting reparations—"blood money"—from Germany. A few months before Eichmann's capture, many Israelis protested Ben-Gurion's decision to meet with Chancellor Adenauer as part of an effort to forge closer diplomatic relations. In America as well, the Holocaust was not absent from the communal agenda. It was commemorated in synagogues, Jewish community centers, and camps. It was even the topic of television shows, including dramas such as *Judgment at Nuremberg* and popular shows such as *This Is Your Life*, which related the life of a Holocaust survivor and her success in America. Novels and memoirs such as *The Wall*, *The Diary of Anne Frank*, *Mila 18*, and *Exodus* were best-sellers and became Hollywood blockbusters.[8]

These findings present us with a conundrum. If there was such extensive discussion and commemoration of the event prior to the trial, why do so many people believe otherwise? Why do many astute observers believe Eichmann's trial precipitated, in the words of Haim Gouri, a "major upheaval"? Why was the editorial board of the leading Israeli newspaper, *Davar*, "amazed" by what it heard at the trial? What was the "sudden and clear realization" that came upon the poet Natan Alterman during the trial? Why did witnesses such as the magistrate Beisky and the Holocaust historian Israel Gutman, as well as the BBC correspondent and long-term Israeli resident Geoffrey Wigoder, insist that the trial brought about dramatic changes regarding the public's attitude toward and knowledge of the Holocaust? Thirty-five years after the trial, Gutman recalled how "the

public here in our country . . . especially young people . . . listened and . . . heard perhaps for the first time what
happened . . . this caused a very strong, a very profound
change in the approach to the average survivors."[9] If there
was already so much attention devoted to the Holocaust,
why did Hausner feel compelled to bring the story of the
tragedy to the world? This was a story he and so many others were convinced had not yet been heard. Somehow all the
publications, commemorations, and popular productions
had not pierced the Israeli national consciousness. And if
it had not pierced the consciousness of the country in which
there were more survivors than any other place in the world,
we should not be surprised that it had not pierced the consciousness of the rest of the world.

Even though the Holocaust had been remembered and
commemorated, never before had it received such consistent
attention. Never had it been on the front pages of newspapers throughout the world, as it was during the trial.
However, it was not just the degree of attention that made
the trial feel so very different to observers. At Nuremberg,
the perpetrators and their documents had been at the center; the victims had barely been a sidebar. Hausner's determination that this trial would be founded on the human
story of the Jewish victims' suffering stands, from a perspective of five decades, as the trial's most significant legacy.
Though the judges, who were exemplary in their conduct
and judgment, dismissed it as of no forensic importance,
they misjudged the lasting impact of this testimony. The
survivors' presence in the witness box moved their intensely

personal stories from the private to the public realm. Many survivors had, of course, told their stories before, but never had such a steady stream of them appeared on an internationally illuminated stage. Through their testimony, what happened to European Jewry was transformed in the public's consciousness. The trial and the debate that followed inaugurated a slow process whereby the topic of the Holocaust became a matter of concern not only to the Jewish community but to a larger and broader realm of people. However, before it could become something that transcended the parameters of the Jewish community, both the event and the people whose lives it had devastated had to be embraced in a far more personal, vivid, and intimate way by other Jews. That process was generated by the trial. It began most palpably in Israel. Moshe Shamir, the novelist and literary editor of *Maariv*, described in 1963 how the trial had transformed the Holocaust from something he saw from outside "the burning house" into a "personal, moral, problem." Leora Bilsky observed many years later that after the trial "abstract knowledge became real" and "history [was] turned into collective memory."[10] In short, as a result of the trial, the story of the Holocaust, though it had previously been told, discussed, and commemorated, was heard *anew*, in a profoundly different way, and not just in Israel but in many parts of the Jewish and non-Jewish world. The *telling* may not have been entirely new, but the *hearing* was. This is where those who have recently documented the extent to which the Holocaust was "present" in postwar Jewish life have missed the mark: they failed to ask whether the information about the Holocaust seeped into a certain Jewish consciousness. Jews knew the basic facts, but they did not construct a full-blown apparatus of memory. Despite the many references to the Holocaust in Israel, America, and elsewhere, the story did not penetrate into their reality the way it did beginning with the Eichmann trial. The new hearing of the history of the Final Solution would shape our contemporary understanding of this watershed event in human history.

In Israel the entire episode—capture, abduction, and trial—had the most immediate impact. It enhanced Israel's conviction that the nation had a legitimate right to represent world Jewish interests. Eichmann's abduction contributed to Israel's sense of "derring-do." As one contemporary commentator boasted, using an idiom of that day, it was evidence of Israel's "moral robustness, and even masculine character."[11] The legacy of Garibaldi Street would ultimately be evident in the Entebbe Airport, at the Iraqi Osirak nuclear reactor, and numerous other places where Israel perceived threats to its citizens. It would also be seen in the late twentieth century, during the struggle to free Soviet Jewry. Israel insisted to Diaspora Jewish organizations that it would take the lead on this matter. It argued that it spoke for world Jewry, particularly Jews in distress.

Ironically, in Israel the narrative of the trial seems to have also generated two contradictory trends simultaneously. It reinforced a Zionist version of history that contrasted Israelis, who were citizens of a sovereign state, with Diaspora Jews, who depended on the benevolence of others for protection. According to this narrative, Israelis could defend themselves and bring those who did them harm to justice; Diaspora Jews could not. Ben-Gurion described the trial as unveiling for young Israelis "the profound tragedy of exile, of dependence on alien mercies, of abandonment to the evil and willful impulse of tyrants."[12] But the trial accomplished something else as well, something that is a polar opposite to this Zionist Weltanschauung. It fostered a different perception of the victims. In Israel and much of the rest of the world, the prevailing impression was that the victims had gone like sheep to the slaughter, and that those who survived had done something untoward in order to ensure their survival.[13] The law under which Eichmann had been tried, the 1950 Nazis and Their Collaborators Law, was instituted in response to grassroots pressure from survivors, not to punish Nazis, but to punish Jews. The Knesset did not adopt the law in anticipation of the arrival of Nazi war criminals in Israel. The intent of the law was to ensure that Jewish survivors who had "collaborated" with the Nazis by serving as Kapos or the like were punished. During the Knesset deliberations, Minister of Justice Pinhas Rosen spoke of the "suspicion and mutual recrimination" among survivors about what they did to stay alive.[14] This began to change as a result of the trial. Before, Alterman, expressing a view regnant in Israel, considered survivors a group that was "separate . . . unfamiliar and anonymous" to the rest of Israeli society. After watching them testify, he came to see them as "an ineradicable part of the nature and image of the living nation to which we belong." Israelis began to comprehend that the victims had not been victims because of some inherent cultural or ideological characteristic. As one Israeli teacher wrote in 1962, "If fate had been cruel to us and we were there—our fate would have been the same as theirs and our heroism no less. The differences do not lie within the nation, but in the 'here and there.' " Israelis increasingly recognized that the distinction between Jews in the Diaspora and those in Israel was not "moral or qualitative," but a matter of a "chronological accident."[15] Haim Gouri made the same observation shortly after the trial:

> Far be it from me to blur the distinction between one who dies without putting up a fight and one who fights back or tries to fight back, because a people who loves life will, by its very nature, always prefer those who try to exact the highest possible price for their own lives. . . . But we must ask the forgiveness of the multitudes whom we have judged in our hearts, we who were outside that circle. And we often judge them without asking ourselves what right we had to do so.

The detailed stories Gouri heard from the witnesses helped him and many others better understand "the state of utter paralysis in which the victims had found themselves the whole time."[16] Dalia Ravikovitz, a young Israeli writer, observed that the trial transformed the Holocaust into "an exploding hand grenade; each of us has been struck by his private splinter. . . ." The testimony of Beisky, Gurfein, Kovner, and Lubetkin-Zuckerman together with that of so many others demonstrated that heroism came in many forms, and that those who went to their death without fighting were not, ipso facto, weaklings. Some Israelis began to grasp that, rather than constituting a different breed of Jews, they were simply generationally and geographically lucky. This was, Leora Bilsky argues, a "crucial step toward developing a more tolerant society in Israel."[17] The recognition that Israelis were not "genetically" different from these Diaspora Jews marked what historian Anita Shapira has described as the initial "step of Israeli identity's long and tortuous path back to the Jewish people." Even though one of the leitmotifs of the trial was that Israelis were a new "breed" of Jew, an increased interest in and even respect for the traditional image of the Jew emerged from the trial. Among the generation of Israelis born in the wake of the establishment of the state, it initiated a "long deferred immersion" in the Diaspora past. The survivors—the witnesses for the prosecution—became a "bridge to the destroyed Diaspora" as Israelis engaged in "reconciliation with the past."[18] These contradictory Israeli reactions— "We are Sabras, who would never let this happen to us," together with "What happened to the victims was simply a matter of chronology and geography"—coexisted in the wake of the trial. Embedded in both these reactions was a deeply pessimistic Weltanschauung, one that perceived Jews as eternal victims who must forever be vigilant about their own fate. It was as if the the verse from *Pirkei Avot*, Ethics of the Fathers, "If I am not for myself, who will be for me?" had been inscribed over the proscenium arch of the Jerusalem theater that had been transformed into a courtroom. For better or for worse—depending on one's perspective—it cemented in the minds of many Jews, particularly in Israel, an "existential fear and suspicion of the outside world" and a reminder, as Hannah Arendt noted, that only those "too weak to defend" themselves fall back when they are threatened on the "compromised phraseology of the rights of man."[19]

In the United States and much of the rest of the Western world, the discourse about the victims took a somewhat different direction, thanks in part to the public's understanding of Arendt's work. Survivors found themselves on the defensive. Scholars took direct aim at them. Bruno Bettelheim universalized his own rather limited and relatively benign experience in a Nazi camp to condemn Jews for "having grown infantile," "grovel[ing]," and then "walk[ing] themselves to the gas chambers." He berated Anne Frank's father for choosing a hiding place with no escape route and glibly declared that their party could have armed themselves "with a gun or two had they wished." Historian Raul Hilberg's theory that centuries of Jewish accommodation with the oppressor had left Jews completely unprepared to deal with the Nazis found added resonance with many people. (Ironically, Arendt, who used much of his work—far more than the Baeck citation—without attribution, thought, what she called Hilberg's "death wish" interpretation of Jews' action was ludicrous.) Survivors seethed with anger at those intellectuals who, despite sitting in safety, knew "exactly how the Jews should have behaved to save themselves."[20] Their responses varied. Some felt hurt and terribly angry. Others decided not to depend on intellectuals to tell their story. Growing numbers wrote their memoirs, turned to Yad Vashem to have their relatives' names listed as among those who perished, and began to speak in schools about their experiences. Over the course of ensuing years, survivors became the driving force in the creation of Holocaust museums and memorials. Those with the means endowed chairs in Holocaust studies at various universities. It would be facile to credit all these developments to the trial alone. Other factors certainly contributed. Survivors, many of whom were teens when the war ended, had by the 1960s and 1970s built families and become rooted in their new lives. Many felt distant enough from the trauma to speak of it, not just to other survivors and their families, but to strangers. Yet it was not just survivors who began to change during this period. The 1967 Six-Day War gave Diaspora Jews a sense of pride in Israel that they had not had before. With it came an increased willingness to speak of why Israel was so crucial to them. The Holocaust was an essential part of that. By this point in time, the Baby Boom generation had come of age. Carrying no sense of guilt for what was and was not done by American Jews during the Holocaust, and looking for a tool to differentiate self-righteously their activist response to the persecution of Jews from what they perceived as their parents' passive response, they delved into the topic. Contrasting their outspokenness on Jewish issues with the supposed "silence" of American Jewry during the Holocaust, they compared the Holocaust to the persecution of Soviet Jewry. Then, in the 1970s, the spectacular success of NBC's *Holocaust* miniseries generated an exponential increase in the "demand" for survivors to speak about their experiences. When one watches the nine-hour saga today it is hard to fathom how such a Hollywood soap opera could have had such an impact, not just in the United States but in Germany, a nation where one imagines there should have been more serious vehicles with which to explore this topography of terror. All this took place in a post-Vietnam America which had begun to make room for and even celebrate the oppressed—African Americans, Latinos, gays, and Holocaust survivors. Even among Jews who disavowed any connection with Israel were those who found the trial had a profound impact on them. Paul Jacobs, a freelance writer who covered the trial for *The New Leader*, described the trial as having forced him "to wonder why . . . the Spanish Civil War was far more important to me" than European Jewry, and why he "did not care as much or as deeply about their fate as [he] had about the fate of the Spanish Loyalists." He also concluded that he "had no right to ask anyone who came out of a concentration camp alive, 'How did *you* survive?' because merely to ask the question was to judge them."[21]

All this combined to create both an increasingly hospitable atmosphere in which survivors might tell their stories, and an audience to listen to them. But it was the trial that began this significant change in their status. As a result of the trial, the one hundred survivors who testified as prosecution witnesses, and by extension all other victims, acquired what Shoshana Felman has so aptly called "*semantic authority* over themselves and over others." Together with that semantic authority came "historical authority."²² Had they previously possessed such authority, the Nuremberg Tribunals prosecutors would not have considered proceeding without them. Yet, though they were not included, contemporary analysts did not consider their absence to have compromised the proceedings. Ironically, much of the testimony at the Eichmann trial would have been more legally appropriate at Nuremberg than it was in Jerusalem.²³ Never had their words received such coverage or been imbued with judicial authority. Some did not invoke that authority until their children asked them to tell their stories. Some worked for years on their memoirs. Some spoke out sooner and some later. But when they did speak out, certain things seemed self-evident. The story they had to tell was of tremendous importance, not just to Jews but to the entire world. They had a unique authority to speak of these matters. And those who had not been there listened in an unprecedented fashion. The Eichmann trial accelerated and, in certain cases, generated a process whereby the private and very personal world of the survivor met the public world of commemoration. Today, as the generation of survivors grows smaller and there are few people left to speak in the first-person singular, it behooves us to pay special heed to an event that gave the victims an enhanced and more authoritative voice and also helped create an "audience" to listen to them in a new and different fashion.

A number of years ago, I was invited to a conference at Yad Vashem. While there, I met a group of young Rwandans who had asked Yad Vashem to train them in how to conduct oral testimonies with trauma victims. They wanted to ensure that the history of the genocide that had decimated their country and their families would be preserved. Yad Vashem, eager to make them feel comfortable, arranged for them to have dinner on their first night in Jerusalem with French-speaking Holocaust survivors. By the end of the dinner, the two groups of survivors had bonded so strongly that the elderly survivors took the young Rwandans under their wings, invited them to their homes, introduced them to their families, and began to build personal relations. One afternoon, I sat with some of the Rwandans outside of Yad Vashem, looking out over the Judean Hills. They told me of their experiences during the genocide, and their meeting with the Holocaust survivors. One young man whose entire family had been murdered said to me: "I want to tell my story and help my fellow Rwanda survivors tell theirs. Just like the Holocaust survivors. I want people to listen to me as they listen to them." Despite the inherent contradiction in his next statement, I completely understood what he meant and recognized the passion with which he said it. I had heard it many times before from Holocaust survivors: *"Les générations futures, ceux qui n'étaient pas là, doivent se souvenir. Et nous qui* étions *là, doivent leur dire*"—Future generations, those who were not there, must remember. And we who *were* there, must tell them.

This may be the most enduring legacy of what occurred in Jerusalem in 1961.

NOTES

Introduction

1. Edward. T. Linenthal, "The Boundaries of Memory: The United States Holocaust Memorial Museum," *American Quarterly*, vol. 46 (Sept. 1994), pp. 421–25; Shoshana Felman, *The Juridical Unconscious* (Cambridge, Mass.: Harvard University Press, 2002), p. 127.

2. The law, under which Zündel was convicted, was eventually declared unconstitutional by the Canadian Supreme Court. *R. v. Zündel* [1992], 2 S.C.R. 731; Second Zündel Trial, *Her Majesty the Queen v. Ernst Zündel* [1988], District Court of Ontario, pp. 45–46, 88, 186.

3. David Irving, "On Contemporary History and Historiography: Remarks Delivered at the 1983 International Revisionist Conference," *Journal of Historical Review*, vol. 5 (Winter 1984), pp. 274–75.

4. *Irving v. Penguin Books Ltd & Deborah Lipstadt*, Day 1 (Jan. 11, 2000), p. 98, www.hdot.org; Deborah E. Lipstadt, *Denying the Holocaust: The Growing Assault on Truth and Memory* (New York: Free Press, 1993), pp. 161–63, 179–81.

5. For judgment in *Irving v. Penguin Books Ltd & Deborah Lipstadt*, see www.hdot.org/en/trial/judgement/13.01.

Chapter 1

1. For the Hebrew text of the announcement, see www.psagot .org.il/index.asp?id=1581.

2. Tom Segev, *The Seventh Million* (New York: Henry Holt, 1991), p. 326; *Maariv*, May 24 and June 3, 1960, in Hanna Yablonka, *The State of Israel vs. Adolf Eichmann* (New York: Schocken, 2004), pp. 33–34, 36–37.

3. Michael Phayer, *The Catholic Church and the Holocaust, 1930–45*

(Bloomington: Indiana University Press, 2000), pp. 165–69; Uki Goni, *The Real Odessa* (New York: Granta Books, 2002), pp. 297, 327–28.

4. Simon Wiesenthal, *The Murderers Among Us* (New York: McGraw-Hill, 1967), flyleaf; Simon Wiesenthal, *Justice Not Vengeance* (New York: Grove Weidenfeld, 1989), p. 70; Guy Walters, *Hunting Evil* (New York: Broadway Books, 2009), p. 332.

5. Wiesenthal, *The Murderers Among Us*, p. 110; Isser Harel, "Simon Wiesenthal and the Capture of Eichmann," unpublished manuscript, available United States Holocaust Memorial Museum, pp. 99–101 [hereafter Harel, "Simon Wiesenthal"]. This manuscript's pages are numbered fitfully. I give page references when possible and relevant.

6. Walters, *Hunting Evil*, pp. 273–74. Though the CIA may have been negligent in pursuing this lead, it did not help Eichmann hide, as some sources subsequently charged.

7. Eli Rosenbaum, *Betrayal: The Untold Story of the Kurt Waldheim Investigation and Cover-Up* (New York: St. Martin's, 1993), p. 451; *New Jewish Weekly*, Oct. 3, 1975, in Harel "Simon Wiesenthal," pp. 25, 30; Simon Wiesenthal to Nahum Goldman, March 30, 1954, in Harel, "Simon Wiesenthal," n.p. Tom Segev's highly sympathetic biography of Weisenthal credits him with having found Eichmann. Segev ignores the fact that, while Wiesenthal had placed Eichmann in Argentina in 1953, in 1959 he believed he was in northern Germany. Had the Israelis followed Wiesenthal's lead, Eichmann would never have been found. Most surprising, Wiesenthal never returned to the baron to find out Eichmann's precise address (Argentina is a large country) or any additional information. Had he done so, Wiesenthal might have actually deserved the credit he is so often given. Even Segev, who paints a highly positive picture of Wiesenthal, acknowledges that this indefatigable Nazi hunter had a somewhat dubious connection to the facts. According to Segev, Wiesenthal "fabricated" information, "snatched [claims] out of thin air," and "shrouded [stories] in a cloud of mystery and fantasy." His assertions were often "figments of his imagination" and "inaccurate." Moreover, he often did this "intentionally." In short, it was not unusual for Wiesenthal to "come out with things that quite simply had never happened." The most telling account of Wiesenthal's connection to the Eichmann capture comes from the Nazi hunter himself. On May 26,

1960, just a few days after the story broke, he told the *Irish Times*, "Personally, I have had nothing to do with Eichmann's arrest." Tom Segev, *Simon Wiesenthal: The Life and Legends* (New York: Doubleday, 2010), pp. 97, 101, 113, 122; *Irish Times*, May 26, 1960.

8. Yehuda Bauer, "Don't Resist: A Critique of Phillip Lopate," *Tikkun*, May-June 1989, p. 67; Elie Wiesel, *And the Sea Is Never Full* (New York: Random House, 1999), p. 129.

9. President's Commission on the Holocaust, *Report to the President* (Washington, D.C.: U.S. Government Printing Office, Sept. 27, 1979), apps. C and D; Jimmy Carter, Executive Order 12169, United States Holocaust Memorial Council, Oct. 26, 1979; Peter Novick, *The Holocaust in American Life* (Boston: Houghton Mifflin, 1999), p. 215; Walter Reich, "The Use and Abuse of Holocaust Memory," www.aei.org/speech/23492.

10. Zvi Aharoni and Wilhelm Dietl, *Operation Eichmann: The Truth about the Pursuit, Capture and Trial* (New York: John Wiley & Sons, 2000), p. 120.

11. Raanan Rein, *Argentina, Israel, and the Jews* (College Park: University Press of Maryland, 2002), p. 165.

12. Harel, "Simon Wiesenthal," p. 4.

13. Tuvia Friedman, *Nazi Hunter* (Haifa: Institute of War Documentation, 1961), pp. 236–43; 244–47; Tuvia Friedman, *The Blind Man Who Discovered Adolf Eichmann in Argentina* (Haifa: Institute of Documentation, 1987); Tuvia Friedman, *My Role in Operation Eichmann: A Documentary Collection* (Haifa: Institute of Documentation, 1990); Neal Bascomb, *Hunting Eichmann* (Boston: Houghton Mifflin, 2009), pp. 119–22.

14. Rein, *Argentina*, p. 165; Peter Malkin and Harry Stein, *Eichmann in My Hands* (New York: Warner Bros., 1990), p. 187.

15. Stan Lauryssens, "The Eichmann Diaries," *Areté*, no. 26 (Autumn 2008), pp. 42, 58.

16. Malkin and Stein, *Eichmann in My Hands*, pp. 190, 200; Aharoni and Dietl, *Operation Eichmann*, pp. 79ff, 146; Bascomb, *Hunting Eichmann*, pp. 232-33.

Notes

Chapter 2

1. Isser Harel, *The House on Garibaldi Street* (New York: Viking, 1975), p. 237.

2. *New York Times*, June 7, 8, 11, 12, 1960; *Time*, June 6 and 20, 1960; Aharoni and Dietl, *Operation Eichmann* (New York: John Wiley & Sons, 2000), pp. 168-69; Raanan Rein, *Argentina, Israel, and the Jews* (College Park: University of Maryland Press, 2002), pp. 176–77; *American Jewish Yearbook*, vol. 62 (1961), pp. 200, 203.

3. Golda Meir, *A Land of Our Own* (New York: Putnam, 1973), p. 134.

4. Hanna Yablonka, *The State of Israel vs. Adolf Eichmann* (New York: Schocken, 2004), p. 45.

5. *La Prensa, El Mundo, La Razón*, all in *New York Times*, June 19, 1960. For the evidence on Eichmann's role in the arrest and deportation of Jews with Argentinean passports, see *The Trial of Adolf Eichmann: Record of Proceedings in the District Court of Jerusalem* (Israel: Ministry of Justice, 1992) [hereafter *TAE*], p. 2362.

6. Rein, *Argentina*, pp. 175, 196–97.

7. National Jewish Archive of Broadcasting, The Jewish Museum, New York, Item T383; Jeffrey Shandler, *While America Watches* (New York: Oxford University Press, 1999), p. 122.

8. *Washington Post*, May 27 and June 25, 1960; *Palladium-Item* (Richmond, Ind.), Feb. 21, 1961, in *The Eichmann Case in the American Press* (New York: Institute of Human Relations Press Pamphlet Series, 1961), p. 13; *Time*, June 20, 1960; *New York Post*, June 2, 1960; *Christian Science Monitor*, June 9, 1960.

9. *National Review*, June 4, June 18, July 2, 1960, April 22, 1961; William F. Buckley Jr., "In Search of Anti-Semitism," *National Review*, vol. 43, no. 24 (1991), pp. 20–62; published as a book by Continuum in 1992.

10. *Haaretz*, July 1, 1960, in Yablonka, *Israel vs. Eichmann*, p. 41; *Washington Post*, June 18, 1960; *New York Times*, June 8 and 18, 1960.

11. *Press Office of German Federal Government*, May 31, 1960; *New York Times*, June 19, 1960; *Washington Post*, May 25, 1960.

12. Raul Hilberg, *The Destruction of European Jews* (Chicago: Quadran-

gle, 1961), p. 119; Norbert Frei, *Adenauer's Germany and the Nazi Past* (New York: Columbia University Press, 2003), p. 55.

13. Yablonka, *Israel vs .Eichmann*, pp. 51–52.

14. *New York Times Magazine*, Dec. 18, 1960, and Jan. 8 and 22, 1961; *Time*, June 13, 1960.

15. Oscar Handlin, "Ethics and Eichmann," *Commentary*, Aug. 1960; Oscar Handlin, "The Ethics of the Eichmann Case," *Issues*, Winter 1961; *Chicago Tribune*, April 14, 1961; Saul Friedländer, *The Years of Extermination* (New York: HarperCollins, 2007), p. xxi; Yosef Gorny, *Between Auschwitz and Jerusalem* (London: Vallentine Mitchell, 2003), pp. 23–25; Elmer Berger, "The Eichmann Case Judgment," (American Council for Judaism, March 28, 1962), p. 20; Erich Fromm, "Israel and World Jews," *Jewish Newsletter*, June 17, 1960.

16. Charles Liebman, "Diaspora Influence on Israel: The Ben-Gurion–Blaustein 'Exchange,' " *Jewish Social Studies*, vol. 36. no. 3 (1974), pp. 275, 278–79.

17. Gorny, *Between Auschwitz and Jerusalem*, pp. 20–27; Carol Felsenthal, *Power, Privilege, and the* Post (New York: Putnam, 1993), p. 68.

18. Herbert Ehrmann, memo to members of the Executive Board and National Advisory Council, July 7, 1960, American Jewish Committee Archives, Irving Engel file 1958-60-61.

19. E. A. Bayne, "Israel's Indictment of Adolf Eichmann," American Universities Field Staff Reports Service, Southwest Asia Series, vol. 9, no. 7 (Oct. 1960).

20. S. Andhil Fineberg to Dr. John Slawson, Dec. 7, 1960, American Jewish Committee Archives.

21. American Jewish Committee, press release, May 1, 1961.

Chapter 3

1. Hanna Yablonka, *The State of Israel vs. Adolf Eichmann* (New York: Schocken, 2004), p. 131.

2. Jacob Robinson, *And the Crooked Shall Be Made Straight* (New York: Macmillan, 1965), p. 210.

Notes

3. Gideon Hausner, *Justice in Jerusalem* (New York: Holocaust Library, 1968), pp. 278–79; Avner Less, "Introduction," *Eichmann Interrogated: Transcripts from the Archives of the Israeli Police*, ed. Jochen von Lang and Claus Sibyll (New York: Farrar, Straus & Giroux, 1982), pp. vii, xxi [hereafter Lang]; Stephan Landsman, *Crimes of the Holocaust* (Philadelphia: University of Pennsylvania Press, 2005), pp. 57–59.

4. David Cesarani, *Becoming Eichmann: Rethinking the Life, Crimes, and Trial of a "Desk Murderer"* (Cambridge, Mass.: Perseus, 2004), p. 23.

5. Ibid., p. 31.

6. Ibid., p. 35.

7. George C. Browder, *Foundations of the Nazi Police State* (Lexington: University Press of Kentucky, 1990), p. 226; Cesarani, *Becoming Eichmann*, pp. 33–35, 39.

8. "Statement Made by Adolf Eichmann to the Israel Police Prior to His Trial in Jerusalem," in *The Trial of Adolf Eichmann* (Jerusalem: Israel State Archives, 1995), col. 63; Heinz Hohne, *The Order of the Death's Head* (London: Martin Kecker & Warburg Unlimited, 1970), p. 334.

9. Hans Safrian, *Eichmann's Men* (Cambridge: Cambridge University Press and Washington, D.C.: USHMM, 2010), p. 19; Lang, pp. 42–47; Cesarani, *Becoming Eichmann*, p. 54.

10. Saul Friedländer, *Nazi Germany and the Jews* (New York: Harper-Collins, 1997), p. 200; Yaacov Lozowick, *Hitler's Bureaucrats* (London: Continuum, 2000), p. 25.

11. Hausner, *Justice in Jerusalem*, p. 293.

12. Samuel Kassow, *Who Will Write Our History? Emanuel Ringelblum, the Warsaw Ghetto, and the Oyneg Shabes Archive* (Bloomington: Indiana University Press, 2007), p. 201.

13. Though Auerbach's department played a crucial role in helping the prosecution, other departments at Yad Vashem were far less successful in doing so. The prosecutorial team expressed frustration with them. Yablonka, *Israel vs. Eichmann*, pp. 73–74; Boaz Cohen, "Rachel Auerbach, Yad Vashem, and Israeli Holocaust Memory," *Polin*, vol. 20 (2008), pp. 213–15; Hanna Yablonka, "Preparing the Eichmann Trial: Who Really Did the Job?" *Theoretical Inquiries in Law*, vol. 1, no. 2 (July 2000), pp. 13–15.

14. *TAE*, pp. 1–8.

15. Hausner, *Justice in Jerusalem*, p. 292.

Chapter 4

1. *Jewish Daily Forward*, April 12, 1961; *New York Times*, Aug. 2, 1961; M. Tsanin, "About the Yiddish Bulletins of the Eichmann Trial," *Jewish Daily Forward*, April 16, 1961, as cited in Jeffrey Shandler, *While American Watches: Televising the Holocaust* (New York: Oxford University Press, 1997), pp. 109, 116.

2. Devin O. Pendas, *The Frankfurt Auschwitz Trial, 1963–1965* (Cambridge: Cambridge University Press, 2006), p. 11; *TAE*, pp. 20–23; Alan S. Rosenbaum, *Prosecuting Nazi War Criminals* (Boulder, Colo.: Westview Press, 1993), pp. 88–91.

3. *Sunday Times* (London), April 16, 1961; *New York Herald Tribune*, April 15, 1961; *The Observer*, April 13, 1961; *Daily Telegraph*, April 19, 1961; all in Gideon Hausner, *Justice in Jerusalem* (New York: Holocaust Library, 1968), pp. 320–21; *Washington Post*, April 30, 1961.

4. *TAE*, pp. 60-61.

5. Ibid., p. 62.

6. Hannah Arendt, *Eichmann in Jerusalem: A Report on the Banality of Evil*, revised and enlarged edition (New York: Penguin, 1994), p. 19 [hereafter *EIJ*]; *New York Times*, April 18, 1961; Haim Gouri, *Facing the Glass Booth* (Detroit: Wayne State University Press, 2004), p. 7; *Washington Post*, April 30, 1961; Moshe Pearlman, *The Capture and Trial of Adolf Eichmann* (New York: Simon & Schuster, 1963), p. 147.

7. *TAE*, pp. 82, 95,101.

8. David Cesarani, *Becoming Eichmann: Rethinking the Life, Crimes, and Trial of a "Desk Murderer"* (Cambridge, Mass.: Perseus, 2004), p. 300.

9. Ibid., pp. 135–38.

10. Ibid., p. 183ff.

11. Ibid., pp. 252–54.

12. Ibid., p. 268.

13. Ibid., p. 67; Hans Safrian, *Eichmann's Men* (Cambridge: Cambridge University Press, 2010), p. 36.

14. *TAE*, p. 285.

15. *Lang*, p. 57; *TAE*, pp. 234–35.

16. *TAE*, pp. 266–68.

17. Ibid., pp. 227–28.

18. Karl A. Schleunes, ed., *Legislating the Holocaust: The Bernard Loesner Memoirs and Supporting Documents* (Boulder, Colo.: Westview Press, 2001), pp. 74–75; Hans Safrian, *Eichmann's Men* (Cambridge: Cambridge University Press and Washington, D.C.: USHMM, 2010), pp. 27–38.

19. *TAE*, pp. 299–300; Yaacov Lozowick, *Hitler's Bureaucrats* (London: Continuum, 2000), p. 63.

20. Hanna Yablonka, *The State of Israel vs. Adolf Eichmann* (New York: Schocken, 2004), p. 89.

21. *TAE*, pp. 323–26, 517.

22. Ibid., pp. 578–79, 584.

23. Ibid., pp. 333–34.

24. Ibid., p. 349.

25. *EIJ*, p. 11; Gideon Hausner, *Justice in Jerusalem* (New York: Holocaust Library, 1968), pp. 176–77; Gideon Hausner, "Eichmann and His Trial," *Saturday Evening Post*, Nov. 10, 1962, p. 59; Yechiam Weitz, "In the Name of Six Million Accusers: Gideon Hausner as Attorney-general and His Place in the Eichmann Trial," *Israel Studies*, Summer 2009, pp. 33, 38.

26. *TAE*, pp.398, 400–01, 412.

27. Ibid., pp. 460–61.

28. Ibid., p. 466.

29. Ibid., pp. 1124–25.

30. Ibid., pp. 640–41; Gouri, *Facing the Glass Booth*, pp. 55–56.

31. *TAE*, pp. 366, 396, 722, 724–29.

32. Ibid., pp. 736, 737, 742, 746–47.

33. Ibid., pp. 748–49, 751; Martha Gellhorn, "Eichmann and the Private Conscience," *Atlantic Monthly*, Feb. 1962.

34. *TAE*, p. 1784.

35. Raul Hilberg, *The Destruction of European Jews* (Chicago: Quadrangle, 1961), p. 529; Randolph L. Braham, *The Politics of Genocide: The Holo-*

caust in Hungary (New York: Columbia University Press, 1994), pp. 465–68, 587–89; Jeno Levai, *Eichmann in Hungary* (Budapest: Pannonia Press, 1961), pp. 69–71.

36. *TAE*, p. 966.

37. Ibid., pp. 1020, 1072; see also Yehuda Bauer, *Jews for Sale* (New Haven: Yale University Press, 1994), p. 168.

38. *TAE*, pp. 1048–50, 1059–60, 1071.

39. Ibid., pp. 964–65, 968.

40. Ibid., pp. 957, 975–86; Braham, *The Politics of Genocide*, pp. 891–93; Levai, *Eichmann in Hungary*, pp. 127–28; Stephan Landsman, *Crimes of the Holocaust* (Philadelphia: University of Pennsylvania Press, 2005), pp. 107–09.

41. *TAE*, p. 1088; Cesarani, p. 185.

42. *TAE*, pp. 1096–97.

43. Ibid., pp. 1111–13; Braham, *The Politics of Genocide*, pp. 957, 967.

44. *TAE*, p. 1114; Levai, *Eichmann in Hungary*, p. 101; Lozowick, *Hitler's Bureaucrats*, p. 265.

45. *TAE*, pp. 1354, 1451; see also Klaus-Michael Mallmann and Martin Cüppers, *Nazi Palestine: The Plans for the Extermination of the Jews in Palestine* (New York: Enigma Books, 2010); and Jeffrey Herf, *Nazi Propaganda for the Arab World* (New Haven: Yale University Press, 2009).

46. *TAE*, pp. 1365–67.

Chapter 5

1. *TAE*, pp. 1420, 1424, 1428, 1478, 1492.

2. Ibid., pp. 1375–77, 1399, 1402, 1416–17, 1431.

3. Ibid., p. 1423.

4. Ibid., pp. 1375, 1431–32; Lang, p. ix.

5. Ibid., pp. 1538, 1525–26, 1541–42, 1567.

6. Ibid., pp. 1538–40.

7. Ibid., pp. 1568; *Time*, June 30, 1961; *The Observer*, June 28, 1961; Haim Gouri, *Facing the Glass Booth* (Detroit: Wayne State University Press, 2004), pp. 167, 191.

8. Ibid., pp. 1381, 1398, 1415–16, 1474–75, 1468.

Notes

9. *New York Times*, June 21, 25, 26, 1961; July 9, 1961.

10. Martha Gellhorn, "Eichmann and the Private Conscience," *Atlantic Monthly*, Feb. 1962, p. 58; Joseph Kessel, in *France-Soir*, July 7, 1961, in Gideon Hausner, *Justice in Jerusalem* (New York: Holocaust Library, 1968), p. 367.

11. Moshe Pearlman, *The Capture and Trial of Adolf Eichmann* (New York: Simon & Schuster, 1963), p. 466; *TAE*, pp. 1575, 1576; Leon Poliakov, "The Eichmann Trial: The Proceedings," *American Jewish Yearbook*, 1963, p. 79.

12. Lang, p. 60; *TAE*, pp. 1602–05.

13. *TAE*, p. 1606; *Washington Post*, July 12, 1961; Heinz Hohne, *The Order of the Death's Head* (London: Martin Kecker & Warburg Unlimited, 1970), pp. 328–30.

14. *TAE*, pp. 1610–11.

15. *TAE*, pp. 1610, 1620–21.

16. *TAE*, pp. 1625–26.

17. Gouri, *Facing the Glass Booth*, p. 108.

18. *TAE*, pp. 1626–27, 1680.

19. Ibid., pp. 1680–81; see also Gunnar S. Paulsson, " 'Bridge over the Oresund': The Historiography on the Expulsion of the Jews from Nazi-Occupied Denmark," *Journal of Contemporary History*, July 1995, pp. 431–64.

20. *TAE*, pp. 1785–87.

21. Pearlman, *Capture and Trial of Eichmann*, p. 466; Poliakov, "Eichmann Trial," p. 79; Harry Mulisch, *Criminal Case 40/61: The Trial of Adolf Eichmann* (Philadelphia: University of Pennsylvania Press, 2005), pp. 52, 141; Gouri, *Facing the Glass Booth*, p. 198.

22. Hausner, *Justice in Jerusalem*, pp. 312, 368.

23. *New York Times*, July 16, 1961; Gouri, *Facing the Glass Booth*, p. 213.

24. Israeli Criminal Procedure Law (Integrated Version), 1982, sects. 175, 176.

25. Omer Bartov, *The Jew in the Cinema* (Bloomington: Indiana University Press, 2004), p. 81; Gouri, *Facing the Glass Booth*, p. 226; *TAE*, pp. 1803–04; Hanna Yablonka, *The State of Israel vs. Adolf Eichmann* (New York: Schocken, 2004), pp. 138–39; David Cesarani, *Becoming Eichmann:*

Rethinking the Life, Crimes, and Trial of a "Desk Murderer" (Cambridge, Mass.: Perseus, 2004), p. 300.

26. *TAE* , pp. 1803–04, 1810–11; Bartov, *Jew in the Cinema*, p. 81.

27. *TAE*, pp.1814–18, 1820.

28. Pearlman, *Capture and Trial of Eichmann*, p. 546.

29. *TAE*, pp. 1826–27, 1829.

30. Ibid., p. 1832.

31. Mulisch, *Criminal Case 40/61*, p. 142.

32. *TAE*, pp. 2047–51, 2061, 2063.

33. Ibid., pp. 2082–84, 2088, 2100–01, 2104.

34. Ibid., pp. 2117, 2122–23, 2137, 2143–44.

35. Ibid., pp. 2130, 2182.

36. Ibid., pp. 2160, 2169, 2178.

37. Ibid., p. 2184.

38. Ibid., pp. 2204, 2216–17.

39. Ibid., p. 2218. In 1988 John Demjanjuk was also sentenced to death under the same law that was used in the Eichmann case. However, his sentence was overturned by the Israeli High Court on appeal in 1993.

40. Tom Segev, *The Seventh Million* (New York: Henry Holt, 1991), pp. 364–65; Yechiam Weitz, "The Founding Father and the War Criminal's Trial: Ben-Gurion and the Eichmann Trial," *Yad Vashem Studies*, vol. 36, no. 1 (2008), pp. 236–37.

41. Avner Avrahami, " 'Maybe' Was Not an Option," *Haaretz*, May 6, 2010.

Chapter 6

1. *Jewish Chronicle* (London), Nov. 1, 1963, p. 1; Konrad Kellen, "Reflections on 'Eichmann in Jerusalem,' " *Midstream*, vol. 9, no. 3 (Sept. 1963), p. 25; John Gross, "Arendt on Eichmann," *Encounter*, vol. 21, no. 5 (Nov. 1963), pp. 66, 68.

2. Hugh Trevor-Roper, "How Innocent Was Eichmann?" *Sunday Times* (London), Oct.13, 1963.

3. Louis Harap, "Notes and Communications: On Arendt's Eich-

mann and Jewish Identity," *Studies on the Left*, vol. 5, no. 4 (Fall 1965), pp. 52–79, in Michael Ezra, "The Eichmann Polemics: Hannah Arendt and Her Critics," http://dissentmagazine.org/democratiya/article _pdfs/d9Ezra.pdf.

4. Stephen Spender, "Death in Jerusalem," *New York Review of Books*, vol. 1, no. 2 (June 1, 1963).

5. "Arguments: More on Eichmann," *Partisan Review*, vol. 31, no. 2 (Spring 1964) pp. 253–83, comments by Marie Syrkin, Harold Weisberg, Irving Howe, Robert Lowell, Dwight Macdonald, Lionel Abel, Mary McCarthy, and William Phillips; Mary McCarthy, "The Hue and Cry," *Partisan Review*, vol. 31, no.1 (Winter 1964), p. 82.

6. Bernard Wasserstein, "Blame the Victim—Hannah Arendt Among the Nazis: The Historian and Her Sources," *Times Literary Supplement*, Oct. 30, 2009.

7. Hannah Arendt, "The Jewish Army—The Beginning of Jewish Politics?" *Aufbau*, Nov. 14, 1941, reprinted in Hannah Arendt, *The Jewish Writings* (New York: Schocken, 2007), p. 137

8. Elisabeth Young-Bruehl, *Hannah Arendt: For Love of the World* (New Haven: Yale University Press, 1982), 328–29; Hannah Arendt, "Answers to Questions Submitted by Samuel Grafton," Hannah Arendt, *The Jewish Writings*, eds. Jerome Kohn and Ron F. Feldman (New York: Schocken Books, 2007), p. 475. Samuel Grafton, a prominent American journalist, was assigned to interview Arendt by *Look* magazine. For a fascinating backstory on why the interview never took place, see Anthony Grafton, "Arendt and Eichmann at the Dinner Table," *American Scholar*, vol. 68, no. 1 (Winter 1999), pp. 105–19.

9. Hannah Arendt, *Eichmann in Jerusalem: A Report on the Banality of Evil*, revised and enlarged ed. (New York: Penguin, 1994), pp. 5, 121 [hereafter *EIJ*].

10. Hannah Arendt to Heinrich Blücher, April 15, 1961, in Walter Laqueur, "The Arendt Cult," *Journal of Contemporary History*, vol. 33, no. 4 (1998), p. 493; Hannah Arendt to Karl Jaspers, April 13, 1961, in Hannah Arendt and Karl Jaspers, *Correspondence, 1926–1969*, eds. Lotte Kohler and Hans Saner (New York: Harcourt, 1992), p. 434; Hannah Arendt to Blücher, April 20, 1961, in Young-Bruehl, *Hannah Arendt*, p. 331.

11. Tony Judt, "At Home in This Century," *New York Review of Books*, vol. 42, no. 6 (April 6, 1995).

12. Alfred Kazin, *Alfred Kazin's America: Critical and Personal Writings*, ed. Ted Solataroff (New York: Harper Collins, 2003), pp. 473–75; Wasserstein, "Blame the Victim,"; Bernard Wasserstein, "Symposium: Is Hannah Arendt Still Relevant?" *Front Page Magazine*, Feb. 26, 2010, http://frontpagemag.com/2010/02/26/symposium-is-hannah-arendt-still-relevant/.

13. Arendt to Jaspers, April 13, 1961, in Arendt and Jaspers, *Correspondence*, p. 434.

14. "Eichmann in Jerusalem: An Exchange of Letters Between Gershom Scholem and Hannah Arendt," *Encounter*, vol. 22, no. 1 (Jan. 1964), p. 51.

15. *EIJ*, p. 3; Elie Wiesel, who covered the trial for *The Jewish Forward*, recalled Arendt's frustration with her inability to understand the Hebrew (conversation with Wiesel, London, Sept. 12, 2008).

16. Arendt to Jaspers, April 13, 1961, in Arendt and Jaspers, *Correspondence*, p. 434; Michael Marrus, "Eichmann in Jerusalem: Justice and History," in *Arendt in Jerusalem*, ed. Aschheim, p. 208; *EIJ*, p. 3.

17. *EIJ*, p. 7; Anita Shapira, "The Eichmann Trial: Changing Perspectives," in *After Eichmann*, ed. David Cesarani (New York: Routledge, 2005), p. 37, n. 9.

18. *EIJ*, pp. 60, 63.

19. Ibid., pp. 116, 125–26.

20. Isaiah Trunk, *Lodzsher Ghetto* [Łódź Ghetto] (New York: YIVO, 1962), pp. 311–12.

21. *EIJ*, p. 119, Shapira, "Eichmann Trial," p. 24; Leora Bilsky, "Between Justice and Politics," in *Arendt in Jerusalem*, ed. Aschheim, p. 234.

22. *EIJ*, p. 123; Primo Levi, *The Drowned and the Saved* (London: Abacus Book, 1986), p. 42.

23. *TAE*, p. 1237; *EIJ*, pp. 223–24.

24. Ibid., p. 119. For the original mention of Baeck see *The New Yorker*, March 2, 1963, p. 42. For the edition in which the "Jewish Führer" phrase was retained, see the 1963 Viking Press edition, p. 105. For Hilberg's original comment regarding Baeck, which Arendt adopted,

adapted, and expanded, see Raul Hilberg, *The Destruction of European Jews* (Chicago: Quadrangle, 1961), p. 292; Segev, *The Seventh Million*, p. 6; Kazin, *Kazin's America*, p. 467.

25. *EIJ*, pp. 11, 61, 254, 274.

26. Ibid., p. 54; Arendt to Jaspers, Dec. 2, 1960, in Arendt and Jaspers, *Correspondence*, pp. 409–10.

27. *EIJ*, p. 27; Arendt to Jaspers, Dec. 23, 1960, in Arendt and Jaspers, *Correspondence*, pp. 414–15.

28. *EIJ*, pp. 259–60, 271.

29. Young-Bruehl, *Hannah Arendt*, p. 361.

30. *EIJ*, pp. 15–17, 18, 38, 200; Norman Podhoretz, "Hannah Arendt on Eichmann: A Study in the Perversity of Brilliance," *Commentary*, Sept. 3, 1963, p. 6.

31. *EIJ*, p. 289.

32. Ibid., p. 91; Christopher R. Browning, *Ordinary Men* (New York: HarperCollins, 1992), pp. 170–71.

33. *EIJ*, pp. 232–33. Arendt seemed not to be aware that Bulgaria's participation in the Final Solution policy was compatible with that of Romania and Hungary (before the German occupation) in that the Bulgarians delivered the Jews residing in territories occupied as a result of World War II to German killing centers while refusing to give up Jews residing within the interwar territorial borders. In other words, they gave up the "foreign" Jews but not the "Bulgarians."

34. Ibid., p. 121.

35. Ibid., pp. 278-79. She subsequently refined this position and explained to a German correspondent that she meant that "no one can be reasonably expected" to share the earth with Eichmann. (Young-Bruehl, *Hannah Arendt*, p. 372); Amos Elon, "Introduction," *Eichmann in Jerusalem*, reprint of 1964 ed. (New York: Penguin Classics, 2006), p. xx.

36. *EIJ*, p. 11.

37. Arendt to Jaspers, Dec. 23, 1960, in Arendt and Jaspers, *Correspondence*, p. 417.

38. Robert H. Glauber, "The Eichmann Case," *The Christian Century*, May 22, 1963, p. 682.

39. Young-Bruehl, *Hannah Arendt*, p. 338; Richard J. Bernstein, *Han-*

nah Arendt and the Jewish Question (Cambridge, Mass.: MIT Press, 1996), p. 159.

40. Kazin, *Kazin's America*, p. 179; Judt, "At Home," p. 5.

41. Arendt to Jaspers, July 20, 1963, in Arendt and Jaspers, *Correspondence*, p. 511.

42. John McGowan, *Hannah Arendt: An Introduction* (Minneapolis: University of Minneapolis Press, 1998), p. 12.

43. Hans Mommsen, "Hannah Arendt's Interpretation of the Holocaust as a Challenge to Human Existence," in *Arendt in Jerusalem*, ed. Aschheim, p. 224.

44. Young-Bruehl, *Hannah Arendt*, p. 345.

45. Hilberg found eighty places that he believed came close to constituting plagiarism. (Raul Hilberg, *Politics of Memory* [Chicago: Ivan R. Dee, 1996], pp. 147–50; 152–57). For additional analysis of the material she used from Hilberg, see Nathaniel Popper, "A Conscious Pariah: On Raul Hilberg," *Nation*, March 31, 2010.

46. Hilberg, *Politics of Memory*, p. 150.

47. Yaakov Lozowick, *Hitler's Bureaucrats* (London: Continuum, 20008), p. 8; Walter Laqueur, "Re-Reading Hannah Arendt," *Encounter*, vol. 52, no. 3 (March, 1979), pp. 76, 79; Christopher R. Browning, *Collected Memories: Holocaust History and Postwar Testimony* (Madison: University of Wisconsin Press, 2003), pp. 3–4.

48. Michael R. Marrus, "Eichmann in Jerusalem," in Aschheim, ed., *Arendt in Jerusalem*, p. 212.

49. Young-Bruehl, *Hannah Arendt*, p. 378.

50. Hillel Tryster, " 'We Have Ways of Making You Believe . . . ': The Eichmann Trial as Seen in *The Specialist*," *Anti-Semitism International*, 2004, pp. 34–42. In an interview Sivan claimed that it was his film which prompted Israel to release the Eichmann memoir in 2000. As one who personally requested the memoir from the Israeli attorney general for use in my trial, I can categorically state that this is at the very best a fanciful claim on Sivan's part. *The Independent*, March 3, 2000, p. 12.

51. Marrus, "Eichmann in Jerusalem," p. 206.

52. *EIJ*, p. 286.

53. Ibid., p. 49.

54. Arendt to Mary McCarthy, May 10, 1961, in *Between Friends*, ed. Carol Brightman (New York: Harcourt, 1995), p. 117.

55. Arendt to Jaspers, June 16, 1961, in Arendt and Jaspers, *Correspondence*, p. 441; Hilberg, *The Politics of Memory*, p. 148.

56. *EIJ*, pp. 229–30.

57. Conversation with Antony Polonsky, June 28, 2009.

58. Arendt to Jaspers, Aug. 6, 1961; Feb. 19, 1966; both in Arendt and Jaspers, *Correspondence*, pp. 445, 628; Elźbieta Ettinger, *Hannah Arendt / Martin Heidegger* (New Haven: Yale University Press, 1995), p. 114.

59. Leora, Bilsky, *Transformative Justice* (Ann Arbor: University of Michigan Press, 2004), pp. 94–95.

60. Alfred Kazin, *New York Jew* (New York: Knopf, 1978), p. 218.

61. Arendt to Jaspers, Oct. 1, 1967, in Arendt and Jaspers, *Correspondence*, pp. 674–75; Arendt to McCarthy, Oct. 17, 1969; Oct. 16, 1973; both in *Between Friends*, ed. Brightman, pp. 249, 349-50.

62. Yosef Gorny, *Between Auschwitz and Jerusalem* (London: Vallentine Mitchell, 2003), p. 45.

63. Notes for a lecture given at Wesleyan University, January 11, 1962, in Young-Bruehl, *Hannah Arendt*, p. 339. Young Bruehl observes that she made this statement before *Eichmann in Jerusalem* was written.

Conclusion

1. Hausner, *Justice in Jerusalem* (New York: Holocaust Library, 1968), p. 452.

2. Though the trial did strengthen Germany's commitment to finding and prosecuting war criminals, some of these investigations, such as the one Lothar Hermann read about in the newspaper, were already in the planning stages prior to the proceedings in Jerusalem. Jeffrey Herf, "Politics and Memory in West and East Germany Since 1961," *Journal of Israeli History*, vol. 23, no. 1 (Spring 2004), pp. 40–64; Mary Fulbrook, *German National Identity After the Holocaust* (Cambridge, U.K.: Polity Press, 2002), pp. 70–71.

3. Tom Segev, *The Seventh Million* (New York: Henry Holt, 1991), p. 361.

4. Hasia Diner, *We Remember with Reverence and Love* (New York: NYU Press, 2009); David Cesarani, "Introduction," in *After Eichmann*, ed. Cesarani (New York: Routledge, 2005), pp. 1–3; Anita Shapira, "The Holocaust: Private Memories, Public Memory," *Jewish Social Studies*, vol. 4, no. 2 (1998), pp. 40–58.

5. Dalia Ofer, "The Strength of Remembrance," *Jewish Social Studies*, vol. 6, no. 2 (2000), p. 37.

6. *Divrei HaKnesset (Records of the Knesset)*, vol. 9, pp. 1655–57; vol. 26, pp. 1386–88; vol. 31, pp. 1264, 1306; vol. 80, pp. 564–66.

7. Boaz Cohen, "The Birth Pangs of Holocaust Research in Israel," *Yad Vashem Studies*, vol. 33, pp. 203–43.

8. For a more complete discussion of the treatment of the Holocaust in American popular culture, see Jeffrey Shandler, *While America Watches* (New York: Oxford University Press, 1999).

9. Haim Gouri, *Facing the Glass Booth* (Detroit: Wayne State University Press, 2004), p. 324; Sidra DeKoven Ezrahi, *By Words Alone* (Chicago: University of Chicago Press, 1980), p. 206ff. The recollections by Beisky, Gutman, and Wigoder are in *The Trial of Adolf Eichmann* [video recording] (Burbank: PBS Home Video, 1997), http://remember.org/eichmann/participants.htm.

10. Jacob Robinson, *And the Crooked Shall Be Made Straight* (New York: Macmillan, 1968), p. 138; Leora Bilsky, *Transformative Justice* (Ann Arbor: University of Michigan, 2004), p. 111.

11. Moshe Prager in *Davar*, May 12, 1961, in Idith Zertal, *Israel's Holocaust and the Politics of Nationhood* (New York: Cambridge University Press, 2005), p. 96.

12. Ben-Gurion quoted in Yechiam Weitz, "The Holocaust on Trial: The Impact of the Kasztner and Eichmann Trials on Israeli Society," *Israel Studies*, vol. 1, no. 2 (Fall 1996), p. 17.

13. Hanna Yablonka, "The Development of Holocaust Consciousness in Israel," *Israel Studies*, vol. 8, no. 3 (Fall 2003), p. 11; Dorothy Rabinowitz, *New Lives* (New York: Alfred A. Knopf, 1976), pp. 18–19.

14. Hannah Yablonka, *The State of Israel vs. Adolf Eichmann* (New York: Schocken, 2004), p. 231.

15. Ibid., p. 165; Hanna Yablonka, "Development," pp. 16–17.

16. Gouri, *Facing the Glass Booth*, pp. 274–75.

17. Ravikovitz in Ezrahi, *By Words Alone*, p. 206; Bilsky, *Transformative Justice*, p. 97.

18. Anita Shapira, "The Eichmann Trial," in *After Eichmann*, ed. Cesarani, p. 33; Alan Mintz, "Foreword," Gouri, *Facing the Glass Booth*, pp. x-xi; Hanna Yablonka, *Israel vs. Eichmann*, p. 162; Bilsky , *Transformative Justice*, p. 102.

19. Yablonka, *Israel vs. Eichmann*, pp. 248-49; *EIJ*, p. 271.

20. Bruno Bettelheim, "The Informed Heart," in *Out of the Whirlwind*, ed. Jacob Landau (New York: UAHC, 1968) pp. 40, 44, 47; Raul Hilberg, *Politics of Memory* (Chicago: Ivan R. Dee, 1996), pp. 154–55; Rabinowitz, *New Lives*, p. 174ff.

21. Paul Jacobs, "Eichmann and Jewish Identity," *New Leader*, July 3, 1961, pp. 14–15.

22. Shoshana Felman, *The Juridical Unconscious: Trials and Traumas in the Twentieth Century* (Cambridge, Mass.: Harvard University Press, 2002), p. 127.

23. In *Irving v. Penguin UK and Lipstadt* my defense team decided not to call survivors as witnesses. We did not want to suggest to the judge that we needed witnesses of fact, which is what survivors would have been, in order to *prove* the existence of the Holocaust. We presented the Holocaust as an established fact that needed no validation. We wanted the focus to be solely on Irving and his lies. Furthermore, since Irving was representing himself, we did not want to subject elderly survivors to a cross-examination, which we feared would be designed by Irving to humiliate and confuse them.

CHRONOLOGY

March 19, 1906 Adolf Eichmann born in Solingen, Germany, part of the Rhineland. His family moves to Austria when he is seven years old.

October 14, 1906 Hannah Arendt born in Hannover, Germany.

1915 Ottoman Empire begins to deport and massacre Armenians. The Armenian genocide, as it was later known, continues for several years, resulting in the displacement and murder of much of the Armenian population of central and eastern Anatolia.

November 2, 1917 The British government, having occupied Palestine, then part of the province of Syria in the Ottoman Empire, issues the Balfour Declaration, promising "the establishment in Palestine of a national home for the Jewish people."

1929   Arab riots in Safed and Hebron, organized by radicals in the Palestinian nationalist movement.

1931   Heinrich Himmler establishes the Sicherheitsdienst (SD) under Reinhard Heydrich; the Schutzstaffel (SS) unit that gathered intelligence on opponents of Hitler both within and outside the Nazi Party.

April 1, 1932   Eichmann joins the Nazi Party in Austria. He joins the SS seven months later.

January 1933   Adolf Hitler is appointed chancellor of Germany.

1933–34   Himmler and Heydrich take over the political police forces, renamed the Gestapo. With the Gestapo's function of combating actual political opponents of the Nazi regime, the SD, still under Heydrich's command and tied to the Gestapo by his leadership, investigates and gathers intelligence on groups of real and perceived opponents of Nazi Germany, including the Jews.

August 1933   After the Austrian government begins a crackdown on the Nazi Party, Eichmann leaves for Germany.

1933   Hannah Arendt, fearing arrest by the Nazi regime, leaves Germany for Paris.

1934 Eichmann applies to join the SD and is accepted.

1935 Hitler issues the Nuremberg Race Laws, depriving German Jews of their citizenship.

1935 Eichmann transfers within the SD to section II 112, which monitors Jewish organizations.

January 1938 Eichmann is promoted to SS-Untersturmführer (SS second lieutenant).

March 1938 German troops enter Austria; Hitler announces that Austria is now united with Germany. Eichmann is transferred to Vienna with instructions to streamline the process of expelling Jews from Austria.

August 1938 Creation of Central Bureau for Emigration of Jews from Austria. Eichmann is in charge of this human "conveyor belt."

November 9, 1938 Following the murder of a German diplomat in Paris by a Jew avenging his parents' deportation from Germany to the Polish border, the Nazi regime conducts a massive, coordinated wave of violence against Reich Jewry. Known as Kristallnacht, the Night of Broken Glass, the event results in the murder of nearly one hundred Jews and the destruction of synagogues and Jewish personal property.

September 1939 Germany invades Poland; Britain and France declare war on Germany.

October 1939 Eichmann orchestrates the expulsion of thousands of Jews and Roma (Gypsies) from Germany, Austria, and Bohemia-Moravia to Nisko, a distant area of Poland where they endure significant hardship. Eichmann implements a previously scheduled deportation transport to Nisko even after Hitler orders a halt to the deportations.

1939–40 With the formation of the Reichssicherheitshauptamt (RSHA), the Reich Main Security Office, Eichmann transfers from the SD (RSHA III) to the Gestapo (RSHA IV).

1941 Hannah Arendt emigrates from France to the United States. Eichmann transfers from RSHA IV D4 (deportations) to RSHA IV B4 (Jewish affairs).

September 1941 First mass gassings at Auschwitz.

November 1941 Eichmann is promoted to
                SS-Obersturmbannführer (SS lieutenant
                colonel).

1941 Former mufti of Jerusalem Hajj Amin al
      Husseini, after participating in a failed pro-
      German coup in Iraq, flees to Italy and
      remains in exile in Italy and Germany until
      the end of World War II.

December 1941 Abba Kovner, leader of the Vilna (Vilnius)
               resistance fighters, calls for active
               resistance against the Nazis.

December 1941 Gassings using vans at Chelmno, Poland.

January 1942 Wannsee Conference, in which RSHA chief
              and SS General Reinhard Heydrich notified
              other Nazi civilian leaders of plans for the
              Final Solution. Eichmann helps prepare
              Heydrich's materials for the conference and
              writes up the minutes afterward.

1942–44 Eichmann, as director of the Reich Main
         Security Office section IV B4 (Jewish
         affairs), organizes the deportations of Jews
         from Europe, with the exceptions of the
         Generalgouvernement, the occupied Soviet
         Union, and Serbia, to killing centers,
         killing sites, and camps.

1944   The Polish-born jurist Raphael Lemkin publishes his *Axis Rule in Occupied Europe*, in which he introduces the word "genocide," which he coined to describe the extermination of an entire people.

March 19, 1944   Germans occupy Hungary. Eichmann arrives accompanied by detachment of a dozen deportation experts with the intent of deporting all the Hungarian Jews to Auschwitz-Birkenau and the Austro-Hungarian border.

April–May 1944   Concentration of Hungarian Jews by Hungarian gendarmerie begins in the provinces.

May 15–July 9, 1944   Hungarian gendarmerie, working with Eichmann's RSHA Special Detachment of SS functionaries, deports some 440,000 Hungarian Jews from Hungary. The vast majority arrive at Auschwitz-Birkenau, where the SS selects about 110,000 for forced labor and sends the rest to the gas chambers. July 7, 1944, Hungarian leader Miklós Horthy stops the deportation of Hungarian Jews. Eichmann helps contravene the order and additional trains are dispatched. (Two final trains are dispatched by Eichmann in August.)

August 18, 1944 As a result of negotiations between
Eichmann and Israel Kasztner, the first of
two transports of Hungarian Jews leaves,
ostensibly for Switzerland. The train is
sent instead to Bergen-Belsen, where its
passengers remain for approximately five
months before they are then dispatched to
Switzerland. Many of the passengers pay
large sums for places on the train.

October 15, 1944 Germans support Hungarian fascist
Arrow Cross coup d'état to overthrow
the Horthy regime in Hungary.
Eichmann returns to Budapest to
organize evacuation of able-bodied
Hungarian Jews by foot to the Austrian
border, from whence the Germans would
deploy them for forced labor. The
conditions of the march and the number
of corpses left on the road induced
Auschwitz Commandant Rudolph
Höss to complain about the brutality.

November 1944 Arrow Cross regime orders a halt to the
evacuation marches. Eichmann returns to
Berlin.

November 1944 Himmler orders the destruction of the
gassing facilities at Auschwitz-Birkenau
after one of them is destroyed during an

armed revolt of the Jewish inmate
Sonderkommandos in October.

May 7, 1945 Germany unconditionally surrenders to
the Allies. Eichmann is captured by the
Allies shortly thereafter.

November 20, 1945 International Military Tribunal at
Nuremberg, Germany, opens. Twenty-
four Nazi leaders are indicted for crimes
against humanity, war crimes, crimes
against peace, and conspiracy.

August 1946 Nineteen Nuremberg defendants
convicted; twelve of them sentenced to
death.

November 29, 1947 United Nations votes to partition
Palestine into Jewish and Arab states.

May 14, 1948 Israel declares its independence.

1950 Eichmann, having escaped from Allied
custody, leaves Germany for Argentina.

1951 Hannah Arendt publishes *The Origins of
Totalitarianism*.

1952 Eichmann's wife and children disappear
from Germany and reappear in
Argentina.

May 1953 Israel establishes Yad Vashem, a national Holocaust museum and research center.

1953 Malchiel Gruenwald publishes a leaflet accusing Israel Kasztner, by then an official of the Israeli government, of collaboration with the Nazis; the government sues Gruenwald for libel on Kasztner's behalf.

June 22, 1955 Judge Benjamin Halevi finds in favor of Gruenwald on most counts.

March 3, 1957 Kasztner is shot by Ze'ev Eckstein; he dies of his wounds shortly thereafter.

January 17, 1958 Israel's Supreme Court overturns Halevi's verdict in Kasztner case, posthumously clearing his name.

May 11, 1960 Eichmann is captured by Israeli operatives in Argentina.

May 23, 1960 David Ben-Gurion announces that Eichmann is in the hands of Israeli security services and will be tried by Israel.

April 11, 1961 Eichmann trial opens in Jerusalem and is broadcast by radio and television around the world.

Chronology

June 20, 1961 Eichmann speaks in his own defense at his trial.

December 11, 1961 Eichmann found guilty by the court.

December 15, 1961 Eichmann sentenced to death.

May 29, 1962 Israel's High Court rejects Eichmann's appeal.

May 31, 1962 Eichmann executed at midnight at Ramle Prison.

February 16, 1963 *The New Yorker* publishes the first of Hannah Arendt's series of five articles on the Eichmann trial.

December 1963 Beginning of the Auschwitz trial, in which twenty-two defendants were tried in Frankfurt. The twenty-month trial was one of many and one of the most publicized trials of Nazi offenders before a West German court.

1979 A presidential order signed by Jimmy Carter establishes the United States Holocaust Memorial Council.

1980 U.S. Congress funds the establishment of the United States Holocaust Memorial Council.

April 1993 United States Holocaust Memorial Museum dedicated in Washington, D.C.

April–July 1994   Hutu-led government of Rwanda massacres an estimated 500,000 members of the Tutsi minority.

November 8, 1994   International Criminal Tribunal for Rwanda (ICTR) established by the United Nations.

July 1995   Bosnian Serbs massacre 8,000 Bosniaks (Bosnian Muslims) in the town of Srebrenica.

September 2, 1998   In the world's first conviction for genocide, the ICTR finds Jean-Paul Akayesu guilty of committing and encouraging others to commit acts of violence in the Rwandan town of which he was mayor.

June 10, 2009   Security officer Stephen Tyrone Johns is killed in the line of duty when the United States Holocaust Memorial Museum is attacked by an anti-Semitic, Holocaust-denying shooter.

June 10, 2010   The International Criminal Tribunal for the former Yugoslavia finds two Bosnian Serbs guilty of committing genocide in Srebrenica in 1995. They are sentenced to life in prison.

ACKNOWLEDGMENTS

I would like to thank those people who read this manuscript or offered observations about the project. They include Benton Arnovitz, Steven Bayme, Havi Ben-Sasson, Peter Black, Richard Breitman, Deborah Dwork, Raye Farr, Shoshana Felman, Jenna Weissman Joselit, Anthony Julius, Maureen MacLaughlin, Antony Polansky, Eli Rosenbaum, Anita Shapira, Ken Stern, and Leah Wolfson. Their contributions made this a better book. Any shortcomings or mistakes are present despite their help. Jonathan Rosen was a magnificent editor who worked with me every step of the way. He has a unique ability to see to the heart of the matter. His passion for the project was infectious. Altie Karper saw this manuscript through the production stage and was most patient with my various delays. Terry Zaroff-Evans did a herculean job of copyediting. Michael Cinnamon did excellent bibliographic research. Maureen MacLaughlin read the manuscript closely and caught many of the errors that invariably find their way into such a work. Carolyn Hessel, who has done so very much for the world of Jewish books, was and is a faithful friend and adviser.

As I noted in the dedication, a portion of this book was written while I was in residence at the United States Holocaust Memorial Museum. Paul Shapiro, the director of the

Acknowledgments

USHMM's Center for Advanced Holocaust Studies, and members of the center's staff, among them Lisa Yavnai, Suzanne Brown Fleming, and Traci Rucker, were all exceptionally helpful and provided a perfect environment for scholarship and research. My special appreciation to the gracious archivist Michlean Amir and to librarians extraordinaire Vincent Slatt and Ron Coleman, all of whom were helpful well beyond the call of duty. They made my time there not only productive but very pleasant. The USHMM's senior historian, Peter Black, carefully read and commented on much in the manuscript. Every conversation with him is a learning experience. This institution is a jewel in our nation's crown.

At my home institution, Emory University, the University Research Committee provided crucial support that helped me complete this topic. Robert A. Paul, the then dean of Emory College, not only granted me a leave but was a wonderful conversation partner. Gary Laderman, the chair of the Religion Department, helped secure important research support. My colleagues were—as always— a delight.

Both the Anti-Defamation League and the American Jewish Committee opened their libraries and archives to me. The director of the ADL's library and research center, Aryeh Tuchman, was gracious and welcoming. Cyma Horowitz of the AJC's library and archives was exceptionally helpful. Her retirement leaves a void that will be hard to fill. The staff of the archives at the Center for Jewish History gave me rapid access to their pertinent holdings. Andrew

Ingall and Aviva Weintraub of The Jewish Museum's National Jewish Archive of Broadcasting helped me retrieve various news broadcasts on the Eichmann trial.

Many scholars have written important works pertaining to the Eichmann trial, among them David Cesarani, Hannah Yablonka, Shoshana Felman, Lawrence Douglas, Leora Bilsky, Hans Safrian, Yechiam Weitz, and Yaacov Lozowick. I have benefitted greatly from their contributions to this topic. Though I have cited their works in my notes, they are deserving of special mention.

ABOUT THE AUTHOR

Deborah E. Lipstadt is Dorot Professor of Modern Jewish History and Holocaust Studies at Emory University. She is the author of *History on Trial: My Day in Court with David Irving* (a National Jewish Book Award winner); *Denying the Holocaust: The Growing Assault on Truth and Memory;* and *Beyond Belief: The American Press and the Coming of the Holocaust, 1933–1945*. She lives in Atlanta, Georgia.